A King

IS
COMING

PAUL WILBUR

WITH PATRICK MCGUFFIN

Endorsements

In this stirring book, world-renowned worship leader Paul Wilbur gives an eye-opening and inspirational charge to the people of God: Look at the Scriptures; look at the increasingly chaotic state of the world; look at the outpouring of the Spirit in the nations, while much of the Church of America slumbers in compromise; look at the rising tide of hatred of Jews and Christians around the globe; look at how God continues to unfold His promises to Israel—and then lift up your eyes, and look to the King in adoration and expectation. He is coming soon!
Dr. Michael L. Brown, host, the Line of Fire radio broadcast
Author of *Answering Jewish Objections to Jesus*

"What on earth is going on?" is a question concerned people ask. "What is God up to?" is a question concerned religious people ask. "What ought I to be about in this earth?" is a question the best of us ask—and here Paul Wilbur does just that. I am pleased to commend Paul Wilbur's timely answers to these questions. *A King is Coming* will definitely get you going—and in the right direction.
Professor Jeffrey Seif

In *A King is Coming*, Paul Wilbur is calling the Church to be the Esther of our day, a people that will stand with God's covenant family when all the nations are turning against her. The last great divide within the Church, the great apostasy, may center around this very issue: those who do not understand God's heart for His Jewish people will be deceived by the world media and culture. Wilbur is urgently challenging the Church to take their stand.

Don Finto
Pastor Emeritus, Belmont Church, Nashville, TN
Founder of Caleb Company

Foreword

We are in a decade when rulership in the earth is being greatly contested. The real issue becomes how and who is aligned with the Ruler of the Nations! Paul Wilbur, who usually takes us into the heavenlies with his worship music, has brought the reality of what the world will be like as the King of all Kings intervenes in society.

Warfare is intensifying around the world. In the midst of warfare, God is saying two things to His people: *"Come up!* Ascend under the shadow of My wing and war from the abiding place I have prepared for you!" and *"Stand still,* cease and desist from striving, and worship Me!" With wars and rumors of wars flying around the world, it is important that as God's people we remind ourselves that we *can* have peace in the midst of the war. The war is a supernatural, spiritual war, not just a war against flesh and blood. We must also remind ourselves that the war is a *worship* war. Who will be worshiped? We declare that our God is worthy to be worshiped!

This is a time for understanding how to overthrow the thrones of iniquity, which is ruling and influencing the earth. God is calling His Church into a new and intimate place where the anointing will break the yoke and overturn the structures holding many captive. God is stirring up His people's faith. He is releasing a gift of faith to break the power of generational, iniquitous patterns, which have stopped families from experiencing the blessings of God. He is empowering people with faith to see His glory spread throughout cities, regions, and states.

The only entity on Earth with the power to break strongholds of the enemy's domain is the Church. The Church must now war to come out of its status quo and into a new structure that presents the gospel to a lost and dying world. Just as the structure was new in the first century, it is being reformed to meet the needs of the world in the twenty-first century. We must change into a vibrant, fire-filled army that marches forward. This call to advance will bring the body of Christ into an energetic worshiping force. This is a time to enthrone Christ as King, so other thrones can be toppled.

In *A King is Coming,* Paul Wilbur helps us meet the challenge for the Church today and transform our way of thinking, so we can truly represent God's Kingdom in the escalating conflict against the kingdom of darkness. Phrased another way, this book helps the Bride put on her war garment and place her "army boots" on the headship of the enemy in every area of society.

Satan's objective is to block the plan of God by establishing his legal right to control an area. Satan gains access into an area the same way he gains access into an individual's life or family line—through sin. He is seeking to escalate individual or family sin into corporate sin. When corporate sin enters into our assigned boundaries, we need to be aware of how that sin can build a throne of iniquity and how we, positioned in God's Army, have the authority to dismantle it. Sin creates a break in God's purpose or order. When this break occurs, Satan takes advantage and begins to establish his influence in an area. From that place of influence, Satan can actually build a throne on which he is seated in a territory. Revelation 2:13 (NKJV) says, *"I know your works, and where you dwell, where Satan's throne is."*

In exalting himself, the enemy is attempting to draw all people to his counterfeit light. He knows that all people are created as vessels of worship, and whether they realize it or not, they will worship someone or something. They will either worship the true and living God, or they will worship Satan and his demonic forces—either overtly or through sin. It is this "worship" of corporate sin that builds the throne on which Satan is seated, and it is from this throne that demonic forces work to perpetuate the sin and establish the throne of iniquity to an even greater extent.

This is the time to go up into the gaps (see Ezekiel 13:5) and block Satan's opportunity. In Luke 11, we find the model for our prayers, a cry for the Kingdom of God to come. The Lord's prayer in the Amplified Bible begins, "*Our Father Who is in heaven, hallowed be Your name, Your kingdom come. Your will be done [held holy and revered] on earth as it is in heaven*" (v. 2). We must invite God to build His Kingdom in our hearts, families, churches, cities, states, and nations. He longs for His Kingdom rule to reside in the earthly realm. It is already here, but not in its fullness. In a sense, it *is already* and it is *not yet*. It is here today, yet still to come in the future.

In order to see God's Kingdom come into its fullness, we must understand how to pray and position ourselves for the future. Get ready for a great shaking! Thrones of iniquity will fall. We are about to see a tremendous shift in worship throughout the world, as God's throne is re-established and the Church rises into a new glory. Join Paul Wilbur as he helps us understand how to watch and pray, because...*a King is coming!*

Dr. Chuck D. Pierce
Vice President of Global Harvest Ministries
President of Glory of Zion International Ministries, Inc.
Denton, Texas

Table of Contents

CHAPTER 1

The War over Our
Minds and over Israel

Have I completely lost touch with reality here, or are you also trying to make sense of the crazy world we live in? Who's driving this thing and where are we all going in such a hurry? The great society of the West, which we have created, supported, even permitted, is spiraling out of control at a dizzying pace. It seems to me that there are no absolutes we can still hold onto as firm in our world anymore—family, gender, marriage, protection for the unborn. As nations lift up their banners of secular humanism and political correctness, why must Bible believers in the West lower theirs? Must God-fearing people also abide by the constantly morphing standards of being politically correct in order to be relevant? We are witnessing a dramatic—no, *critical*—shift in our national moral and social compass that will take us down a path I fear may be unrecoverable in just a few short years.

Have you wondered why Iran and her terrorist pawns are so hell-bent on destroying Israel? Maybe you have noticed that the Obama administration yanked its commitment to Israel, once considered our most loyal and important ally? As I write this, Palestinian Arab terrorists have launched over three hundred attacks on Israeli citizens and have literally stabbed innocent civilians, including women and children, with kitchen knives. Many nations have tried to use the United Nations Security Council against the State of Israel. This is a renewed attempt to force Israel into the dangerous position of giving up key concessions before negotiations can begin and mandating that Israel accept indefensible borders. But why is this happening now? Is there a more diabolical plan behind what we are hearing and experiencing in today's headlines?

Day in and day out, there are signs and signals all around us that indicate, and even foretell, events to come. Traffic signs deliver important messages that try to keep us from a potential tragedy. Observing signs in nature can help us predict upcoming changes, like buds on a bare tree branch can signal that springtime is just around the corner, or dark clouds mixed with heavy wind can warn of an approaching storm.

In business, investment strategists watch for specific signals helpful in predicting downturns in the economy. Parents watch for certain tendencies in their children, as they seek to help mold their character. National governments carefully study the movements within other governments in order to position, protect, and secure their own borders and futures. Critical signs are erupting all around us, some even conveying world-changing implications for the future. *But are we paying attention?*

What do these signs mean? What do they signal?

Terrorism is taking center stage on the news, yet most people have no clue how widespread it actually is. According to Statista, between 2006 and 2013, there have been approximately 130,000 fatalities, resulting from approximately 90,000 separate terrorist attacks. Really? Yes, really!

But even if we ignore current world affairs, how can we ever forget our own nation's heart-cry on September 11, 2001, when hijacked planes slammed into the World Trade Center in New York, the Pentagon, and a field in Pennsylvania, resulting in 3,000 deaths and 8,900 injuries? And how about 780 terrorism deaths in Nigeria in 2009, 331 deaths resulting from bombs on Air India flights, 170 deaths with 656 injuries in a Moscow theater, and 137 deaths and 352 injuries in the restaurant and theater bombings in Paris? When and where will it all end?

So many are asking why? But perhaps the real question should be "what"—*what does all this mean and what are these signs trying to tell us?*

Society's moral compass is spinning out of control, no longer pointing people to true north. It occurs to me that the clear founding principles of the United States, and its Judeo-Christian roots, have somehow become a free-for-all stew, with indistinguishable ingredients and tastes. No longer are key foundational elements of society viewed as solid anchors. Instead, we are blown around by the changing winds of our time. Traditional values have been scorned and replaced by the non-values of relativism, deference, and human secularism.

Nowadays, even marriage has been relegated, by law, to become a haven for relativism! It is no longer viewed as being a God-given institution between one man and one woman. Marry who you will, because "anything goes." Convenience has replaced the value of life in protecting the unborn. If an unplanned pregnancy is an obstacle for your career path, end the life. Of course these statements alarm me deeply, as I consider the depths to where our nation has fallen. I simply say this because much of our society has adopted these distorted views without even a second thought. The idol of self-orientation and self-fulfillment has been raised over God's truth.

Unfortunately, these views have permeated throughout every fiber of our society. Prayer to the Creator and Sustainer of life was banned from our schools in the 1970s, but that was just the beginning. Now our governmental institutions and military are being forced to abandon their beliefs, as praying to the God of Abraham, Isaac, and Jacob has become an offense. Businesses that stand on their Judeo-Christian beliefs are persecuted and prosecuted in our courts and marketplace. People who declare what God's Word says about these issues are labeled "extremists" and "haters." In fact, some have been charged with what is now called "hate crimes." Government officials, with God-honoring convictions, who refuse to marry homosexuals are tossed out of their jobs, losing their ability to provide for their families. If that isn't bad enough, they now carry that label to their future hopes for employment. Christians who feel morally bound by their religious convictions to not support ungodly lifestyles are now forced to do so by law. In our haste to not offend the few, we are willing, rather, to offend the many and even God Himself, if need be!

Is there a message amidst all of this craziness that God is trying to expose to those who have eyes to see, ears to hear, and hearts to discern? What do all these signs indicate? How do we detect the message hidden within the revolution of Western society? Noah, Daniel, Josiah, Jonah…where are you guys? We need you!

A war for the throne!

There is a war raging that targets the minds of the people in our nation and the nations of the world. We speak about terrorism with its fatalities and casualties in the physical realm, but the mystery that most remain oblivious to is the war fomenting all around us—the war for our minds. There are unseen forces that desire to manipulate our thinking and decision-making. Ultimately, this is a war of biblical proportions; it is the clashing of kingdoms from before time began. This is the battle that John saw as he wrote the book of Revelation—this is for *all* the marbles—winner takes all!

Yet this is no game. No, it is an all-out war for Jerusalem, the city of the Great King, and the throne of almighty God.

In a desperate attempt for control, ungodly people push their agenda, while God-fearing people sometimes find themselves doubting their faith and resolve. But the stakes couldn't be higher! There is a King coming who has indisputable rights to this throne and another who desperately wants to take it away. This battle for the throne often finds its main battleground in our minds, seeking to control our resulting actions—individually and as a nation.

As evil has attempted to take control, political correctness has become a higher value in the USA than righteousness and truth. Right and wrong are consistently being redefined to cater to certain special interest groups. Companies today will pay a huge price if they go against the LGBT (lesbian, gay, bisexual, and transgender) agenda, including possible crippling legal fees if they choose to stand on biblical standards. As I alluded to earlier, disagreeing with the new norms of our society has now been labeled "hate." No longer are you allowed to debate the leading moral issues of our day without being called a hater (or being ridiculed on social media)—complete with potential lawsuits under hate-crime legislation. Am I out of touch with reality, or have we not entered into the days when men are calling good *evil* and evil *good*?

Do I have your undivided attention yet? I certainly hope so!

This downward spiral began when godly people refused to say anything as others violated God's clear direction, revealed in Scripture. Bible-believing and God-fearing people remained silent, and society interpreted that silence as a condoning of this type of activity and belief system. We must realize our silence is highly destructive to the purposes of God. Slowly, but surely, this aggressive, radical agenda began to filter into the Christian culture. Mixed seed began to be sewn in our nations and in our houses of worship. The loudest and wealthiest, which have spent the most money promoting their agendas, began to win the hearts and minds of the undiscerning masses, and they were easily swayed. Our children were slowly re-educated, indoctrinated, and then enlisted. Yes, they were re-educated to adopt and adapt to the ways of our new society—the new norm! As these kids grew up, they continued the re-education process with their own children.

If this all sounds a little too "cloak and dagger" for you, simply consider the attitude shift with regards to family, country, life, liberty, God, and right and wrong between the major generational groups of our day. Consider as a group the "Greatest Generation" of WWII (mostly gone now), the "Baby Boomers" of the 1950s and 1960s, the Gen Xers, and finally, the Millennials. Their views concerning the most basic aspects of life—God, success, fairness, and so on—have each taken noticeable, if not radical, turns from what would be considered a "conservative right of center" position to a strongly "far left of center," socialistic view of society.

Recently, a friend brought me a book copyrighted in 1930 entitled *HUMANISM: A New Religion*. On page 128, Charles Francis Potter states:

> Education is thus a most powerful ally of Humanism, and every American public school is a school of Humanism. What can the theistic Sunday schools, meeting for an hour once a week, and teaching only a fraction of the children, do to stem the tide of a five-day program of humanistic teaching?

Yes, this was written in 1930! As we look at what has happened in our own lifetime, with our own children and grandchildren, and even to *us* to a certain extent, I ask you, was the author's pronouncement truly prophetic? You tell me! Have our school systems, governments, arts, entertainment, and news sources been hijacked by a godless movement? Were we not warned that in the last days men would reject sound doctrine and teaching in order to embrace the things they wanted to hear? Are we finally there? This far left of center agenda knows that with God out of the picture, you can persuade just about anyone to do just about anything and convince them that it's good and right.

So why is all this happening now? It is because…

a King is coming!

This is, in fact, the hidden mystery behind the headlines of our day! These signs and events signal the return of the King of Kings—Yeshua, our Messiah! Jesus Christ, King of Kings and Lord of Lords will triumphantly and physically return to Earth, and every eye will see and every mind will grasp the truth, that He *alone* rules.

But we must remember and understand that the enemy of life—veiled as a chameleon that appears as one color, but can easily morph into another—has convinced this world that God is out of the picture and that the Bible is archaic, out of touch, and irrelevant. Satan's agenda is to deny the fact that the King of Kings—Yeshua—is soon to appear, and then Satan will try to convince the world that *he* is supreme ruler. The old adage is still true: Tell a lie often and loud enough, and it will be viewed as the truth.

And that reminds me...

When I was fresh out of college, I had friends who loved to sail and compete in friendly neighborhood regattas (racing their sailboats on the Long Island Sound). The weather on the Sound is notorious for being finicky and unpredictable, because the water there is shallower than you might expect. One particular day when we began the race, the sky was clear and the water pristine; but as we rounded the third mile marker, the sky turned an ominous black, and the winds picked up speed. The captain seemed to be undaunted by the signs and told the crew that it was just a small aberration in the weather and certainly nothing our 37-footer couldn't handle with ease.

Well, so much for the captain's analysis. The winds picked up to 35-40 mph gusts, tearing our jib and ripping the mainsail, threatening all hands on board. Our lines jammed as we attempted to lower the sails, and something had to be done before we capsized in the angry seas. Not knowing any better, I grabbed a knife and placed it between my teeth. I scaled the aluminum mast in my skivvies during a lightning storm, cut the lines free and returned to the deck in one piece. Even then, the Lord was watching over my foolish ways because He knew my end from the beginning!

The lesson here is pretty simple: The signs were there to be discerned, but the captain didn't have the eyes, nor humility, to see them. No one prepared for the potentially devastating storm, and as a result, there was a lot of damage to the boat, along with the great risk of life. Notice the use of the word *humility* in this lesson learned. I chose that word carefully because only a humble man will receive instruction, take note of the signs, understand the message, and be saved from disaster.

Scripture is loaded with prophecies, describing times such as these as the preamble to the return of God's Messiah. But to most, the events and culture of the day tend to cover or shield heaven's great announcement. People are so consumed with themselves that they misinterpret, or even fail to see, the signs of the times as being the foreshadowing of the great and terrible Day of the Lord, as proclaimed in the following Scripture:

You will hear of wars and rumors of wars, but see to it that you are not alarmed. Such things must happen, but the end is still to come. Nation will rise against nation, and kingdom against kingdom. There will be famines and earthquakes in various places. All these are the beginning of birth pains. (Matthew 24:6-8)

Yes, the planet is experiencing the initial birth pains, announcing the return of our King Yeshua! Consider what the apostle Paul foretold in 2 Timothy 3:1-5:

But mark this: There will be terrible times in the last days. People will be lovers of themselves, lovers of money, boastful, proud, abusive, disobedient to their parents, ungrateful, unholy, without love, unforgiving, slanderous, without self-control, brutal, not lovers of the good, treacherous, rash, conceited, lovers of pleasure rather than lovers of God—having a form of godliness but denying its power.

Now come on, doesn't this sound like people today? Didn't Paul just nail it when he prophesied over two thousand years ago about our current culture?

There is truly a greater, hidden message behind what we are seeing today! Signs are supposed to point us to something, to warn us, to inform us, to protect us, to help us negotiate life successfully. The signs of the times in which we live are meant to be a display of

God's grace, pointing us to the fact that His Son, Jesus, King of Kings, will soon return. In His great kindness to a self-absorbed world, He is exposing these many signs of the times to those who have eyes to see and ears that *still* hear.

Seeing these signs and signals, and understanding that a King is coming, will help us interpret the events of the day. Hopefully, we will pause to consider how we are living and adjust accordingly. No longer are we left to wonder what is going on. These are His signals that we must prepare for His return!

But along with this exciting news that the King is coming, we must be aware that with the ease of modern communication, the world is exploding with information. Nearly everyone has a personal communication device or at least access to the Internet. Multiple streams of information are flowing in compelling and provocative ways. There is mass input, requiring everyone to decide which of the competing voices holds the truth. In other words, there is—in the truest sense of the word—a "war" over our minds, thoughts, desires, decisions, and especially our resulting actions.

So, wake up!

This is an incredible time in history to be alive. A King is coming…and most aren't prepared, Christians and non-Christians. The non-Christians are not prepared because of their lack of acceptance of God's one and only provision for salvation. Tragically, they will find themselves living forever in a horrible place, which God created for the rebellious angels/demons that rejected God's rulership of all. And, at the same time, many Christians continue to go about living self-absorbed lives, the same as unbelievers, ignoring the signs Jehovah has given. Their friends, families, and God's purposes are currently taking a backseat to their selfish yearnings.

It is time to wake up from our slumber and realize that a King is

> The signs of the times in which we live are meant to be a display of God's grace, pointing us to the fact that His Son, Jesus, King of Kings, will soon return.

coming! There is a call of God on our lives to strategically participate with Him in His purposes today. Our failure to see and understand the signs will not be a good enough excuse. To not engage in the battle is no longer an option. In this battle for the throne, either you win...or you die!

CHAPTER 2

A Planet in Crisis—Past the Tipping Point?

The mystery has been revealed. A King is coming, yes...*the* King is coming! All the signs point toward this ominous event in our planet's history. And with our world in a *spiritual identity* crisis, it begs these questions: Are we past the tipping point? Are we lowering the life boats, and is the band playing "Nearer My God to Thee" on the promenade deck?

There comes a point when a ship has taken on so much water that it moves past merely tipping and begins the horrible, irreversible process of submerging. Commonly, this is referred to as the *tipping point*. This concept is used to describe a critical point in businesses, marriages, families, and even nations. But I wonder, can it also be used to describe a point in history for an entire planet? Assuming for a moment the answer to that question is yes, what are the signs of a culture taking on so much "water" that it nears the point from which there is no escape or recovery?

When people consider God to be "out of the picture" or irrelevant, they will likely come up with an answer to this tipping point question, which is very different from a believer's point of view. They likely would note that problems can be dealt with according to human abilities and reason, and therefore the "weight" of the water can be shifted temporarily, giving the impression that the ship has been correctly righted and lives have been protected.

But with God clearly in the picture of sustaining this world He created (see Hebrews 1:3; Colossians 1:17), an entirely different standard will be used to determine when and how our nation passes the tipping point threshold of mercy and grace and begins to invite the judgment of God instead. Remember a couple of cities called Sodom and Gomorrah…Babylon, Nineveh? *Selah.*

A ship is not designed to take on more water than the hull is capable of displacing. By the same token, a nation such as the United States of America, founded upon certain Judeo-Christian principles, can only offend God to a certain point of His mercy before it moves into making a mockery of God—and God will not allow Himself to be mocked. The apostle Paul assures us in Galatians 6:7, *"Do not be deceived: God cannot be mocked. A man reaps what he sows."* Since a man reaps what he sows, is it also possible that a people, a culture, or even an entire nation will reap what they sow as well? We are a planet in crisis, but have we passed the tipping point?

Since a man reaps what he sows, is it also possible that a people, a culture, or even an entire nation will reap what they sow as well?

Both Psalm 14:1 and Psalm 53:1 agree when they state: *"The fool has said in his heart 'there is no God.'"* The Hebrew word for fool used in both verses is the word *naval.* It does not refer to a stupid or ignorant man, but rather, the definition speaks of a man who is "morally and spiritually devoid of truth; bankrupt in his soul." So if the elected leaders of a city, state, or nation are devoid of moral and spiritual truth, can there be any hope for the people they govern?

I typically travel over three-hundred thousand miles a year and minister on almost every continent each year. I see wonderful, yet hurting, people all over the world, and still America has continued to be the recipient of God's favor. Why? Well it's not because we are smarter, more beautiful, or more deserving, I assure you. There are incredible people all over this planet who are as smart, good-looking or every bit as brilliant as many in the USA. (I know I am not in the front of that line!)

Two giant pillars have propped up America. These pillars to this great nation have served as our protection and stability and have supported God's rich favor upon America and its people. So what are these pillars, these guardian angels that have held up our nation, invited the blessing of God and preserved us in the face of adversity, depression, world wars, and disasters over the past several generations?

The first pillar that supports our nation is the propagation of the salvation message through Jesus Christ—the gospel. We have been actively receiving and spreading the gospel of salvation in Jesus within our borders and throughout the world. We have invested more time, resources, manpower, and prayer into the preaching of the gospel than any other nation in history. Until recently, America has been viewed in the eyes of its own and those of the world as a Christian nation. We express the attributes of Christianity in the world—we help the helpless, feed the hungry, assist in times of disaster, sacrificially come to the aid of our allies, promote religious and political freedom, and above all, spread the hope found solely in Jesus the Messiah. Although we were founded on the guiding principle of religious liberty, that expression has been primarily found in promoting the Judeo-Christian faith proclaimed in the Bible, and because of that, God has smiled on us as a nation.

The spread of God's plan of salvation for all mankind has been broadcast throughout the world by Americans in many ways. Bibles were translated, printed, and shipped around the globe and were even carried by loving Christians behind the infamous Iron and Bamboo Curtains. Missionaries and evangelists were raised up, trained, funded, and sent to the ends of the earth. Christian schools and universities educated hundreds of thousands of ministers, built churches, and set up missions across the planet. Christian student movements filled our high schools and universities. And did you know that college fraternities, now famous for parties and hazing new members, were originally established as Christian clubs for fellowship and Bible study? While in school, I joined one such fraternity called Alpha Tau Omega. You don't need to be a brain surgeon to figure out the original vision for this band of brothers, now do you? Christian media—including music, books, publications, television, radio, and video—crisscrossed the continents. Christian businessmen and businesswomen formed powerful world-changing organizations to infiltrate and impact the business world and the marketplace. People put their faith into action and sacrificially gave billions of dollars, and their lives, to thrust forth the Kingdom of God all over this planet. And so I believe that it is all of these efforts, and more, that have sustained us as a people and have strengthened the "everlasting arms" that supports the great country of the United States of America.

The second pillar that has supported our nation and invited the blessing of God has been the United States' history of standing with the nation of Israel. Until recently, America had been an unwavering strong ally of the State of Israel in the face of growing international anti-Semitism and massive Muslim armies dedicated to wiping her off the face of the earth. Israel's greatest allies, supporters, and funding mechanisms, have been the Jewish and Christian people of America.

The people in our Judeo-Christian nation share religious roots with the Jewish people, as well as a God-given plan and purpose for the establishment of our nations. The Jewish people were finally gathered back into their ancestral homeland on May 14, 1948, when the State of Israel became the first Jewish nation in nearly two thousand years. Listen to a few of the final words recorded by the prophet Isaiah in chapter 66, verse 8:

Who has ever heard of such a thing? Who has ever seen such things? Can a country be born in a day or a nation be brought forth in a moment? Yet no sooner is Zion in labor than she gives birth to her children.

The prophet Ezekiel also saw this same event in his famous "dry bones" vision and prophesy in chapter 37. One of my favorite songs that I co-wrote takes its words and inspiration from this amazing prophet of God.

I hear the sound of a prophet, declaring the word of the Lord
I hear the voice of Ezekiel, prophesying to these dry bones

Live again, live again
To those who are sleeping
To those in the grave live again...

I hear the sound of an army, a nation preparing for war
I can hear Judah assembling:
Praise is their weapon of war.

Live again, live again
To those who are sleeping
To those in the grave live again...

Breath of God from the four winds blow
Breathe life again, to these dry bones

Arise, Arise, Arise, Here and now, O arise!

I hear the voice of the watchman, cry from his place on the wall.
Awaken the remnant of Zion, salvation for all Israel!

Live again, live again
To those who are sleeping
To those in the grave, live again!
Raise up an army, Raise up an army
Raise up an army, From the dust of the earth

Raise up an army, Raise up an army
Raise up an army of worshipers

Arise, Arise, Arise, Here and now
O Arise!

These two pillars—propagating the gospel of salvation and supporting the nation of Israel—have caused the United States to be blessed. The vision of these two pillars and the understanding of what they are came to me while I was in prayer several years ago. While praying for our country, I saw an old-fashioned scale appear in my mind's eye, the kind that Lady Justice holds while blindfolded. Standing next to the scale was a long line of people waiting to be weighed. There were two great counterweights on the other side of the scale by which the people were judged. As the full scene came closer into view, I could see writing on the counterweights; they each had a name. On the first was written: "The blood of my Son" and on the second was inscribed: "The blood of my firstborn." When I asked what this all meant, I got the impression that the line of people were not individuals, but they represented nations. The nations were being weighed and judged by the two counterweights. The first counterweight asked, "What did you do with the blood of my Son; how did you treat the gospel, which I gave for your salvation?" And the second counterweight asked, "What did you do with the blood of my firstborn; how did you treat the Jewish people that I sent you as another testimony of my faithfulness?"

In other words, if you want to know if you are living in a *sheep* nation or a *goat* nation, you simply need to be able to have an honest answer to the two sets of questions above. According to Matthew 25, there will be a judgment of the nations, and Jesus will separate the *sheep* nations from the *goat* nations. Blood is very important to the whole story here. First, the life of the flesh is in the blood and it is necessary for forgiveness (Leviticus 17:11). Second, blood has a voice. Righteous Abel's blood was crying out against his brother Cain from the ground (Genesis 4:10), and the blood of Messiah Yeshua will judge all mankind. Third, you must have blood in order to make a blood covenant. According to God almighty, this is the strongest kind of agreement in the universe (Hebrews 9:12-14).

Armed with this information, it should give any sober person great pause when considering their country's history and present-day attitude toward the so-called "separation of church and state" and how zealously one pursues eradicating anti-Semitism. It occurs to me that with the current atmosphere in the United States, at any moment, these two mighty pillars, which America has valued for generations, could give way. I believe these two honored sentinels have enabled our nation to walk in the favor of almighty God, and yet the cracks they have sustained in only the past twenty years have so significantly and deliberately weakened the United States, that at any moment, they could crumble as we reach the tipping point. The tipping point I speak of here is no laughing matter; it is the place where God's grace begins to withdraw and His judgment ensues.

To make my point even more clear, let's consider the facts. Somehow with the economic collapse of other nations, the United States has escaped deep financial losses. Interest rates for homebuyers are at a new fifty-year low as I write these words, and there is no massive Jewish exodus from our country, like France and Russia are experiencing.

To right the ship of our nation will take absolutely nothing less than an act of God. It will also take an about-face of a passive Church that repents as well as passionately and aggressively pursues the fruits of love and righteousness. Before we get all overwhelmed and depressed, let's remind ourselves that this wouldn't be the first time a nation was situated where America currently finds herself today. God has provided a formula, which if applied, can turn the onset of His righteous judgment and once again invite His blessing.

King Solomon received this wisdom from God and had it recorded in 2 Chronicles 7:14:

"If my people, who are called by my name, will humble themselves and pray and seek my face and turn from their wicked ways, then will I hear from heaven and will forgive their sin and will heal their land."

God gives a conditional promise—an "if" requirement, followed by a "then" result. First, America must humble herself enough to seek the one true God in contrite communication, known as prayer, followed by true repentance. Second, this nation must decide and follow through with the decision to turn away from its wicked ways, as God defines wickedness. It is only after these two conditions are fully in place that God will hear from heaven, forgive our sin, heal our land, and restore His blessing.

Also, did you happen to notice where the responsibility lies with the conditional promises of 2 Chronicles 7:14? The opening line says "If *my* people..."—not the guy next door, the mayor, senator, or even president of the whole bone pile! No, we were never intended to be a passive subculture within a greater social structure just passing through the mess! On the contrary, we were intended to be a radical counterculture that effects change through righteous judgment, voting our conscience, speaking out against destruction, and living a life that is worthy of the calling we have received!

Believe it or not, most people I come across, consciously or subconsciously, don't believe God intends to carry out what He says. Even though we were created in God's image, He is not like us. What He declares in His Word, He will enact. His integrity of delivering upon His promise is 100 percent guaranteed, and He has *never* spoken a word that He has not fulfilled. His words and actions are of an exact measure and carry an equal weight. He declares Himself to be the great I AM—the One who speaks and all creation obeys.

And yet, sadly, most people don't give God's words the weight they deserve, perhaps hoping that almighty God will always relent on His righteousness and justice. Time and time again, believers and unbelievers act as if they don't understand there are consequences to personal actions of disobedience, as well as consequences for not taking actions when clearly commanded to do so. This applies to nations as well.

When the United States' highest court decided to redefine marriage to include same-sex unions, most people did not share God's offense; maybe that's because this action didn't affect them personally...yet. Maybe some expressed disgust, but they soon joined the vast majority of Christian pastors and remained silent. What is truly bewildering to me is that some of the more liberal sects of Christianity have embraced the new edicts with joy. They are celebrating by giving those who are living the LGBT lifestyle positions of authority in their churches, allowing them to administer, admonish, and uphold the *rest* of Scripture in their respective denominations! Furthermore, if you haven't noticed, the good old fashioned "silent majority" has been silent for so long that they are now legally marginalized as a matter of law. And political correctness? It now requires more than silence— it requires all of us to conform to what God calls an abomination. Scripture clearly discusses this in detail in Romans, 1 Corinthians, and Leviticus, as well as many other places. But because the culture has been so indoctrinated over the years, sin is not considered the problem any longer. Scripture is now considered, or viewed, as the problem. Well, maybe not all of Scripture—maybe just that mean, ol' apostle Paul. Wasn't he single? Wasn't he taught by that Old Testament Jewish scholar Gamaliel? How could he possibly understand human sexuality, especially in this modern enlightened era?

If you are concerned by how the nation has adopted a lesbian, gay, and bi-sexual agenda, then I guess you are really blown away by what is happening in our nation with the agenda of pushing transsexuals in our schools, government, and public washrooms. Oh, and lest we forget, this expanded agenda has propelled past mere public institutions and is now being mandated on the business community at large. The old adage that if you let the nose of the camel in your tent, you better expect the rest of the camel to come in shortly, is true on this downward spiral in our society. The passive Church now is seeing men and boys in girl's restrooms, women and girls in boy's restrooms, and "transgenders" given equal footing anywhere they so choose. Are you and your children feeling safe yet?

The Boy Scouts of America (BSA) have now embraced homosexual boys and adult leaders. Forget that the Boy Scout law says: "A scout is trustworthy, loyal, helpful, friendly, courteous, kind, obedient, cheerful, thrifty, brave, clean, and *reverent*." Since its inception, members of the BSA have repeated the Scout Oath, which declares: "On my honor, I will do my best to do my duty to God and my country and to obey the Scout Law; to help other people at all times; to keep myself physically strong, mentally awake, and *morally straight*." So being "morally straight" is a key character trait affirmed and implanted by the Boy Scouts. In fact, doesn't the LGBT agenda use the word "straight" to describe a life that is in contrast to a "gay" lifestyle?

How long do you think it will be before the BSA is forced to drop the reference to *God* in their oath, if it hasn't already happened by the time you read these words? I find it very ironic that there is so much zeal for changing definitions of words like "straight," "marriage," "sexuality"—all in order to accommodate and excuse dangerous and destructive behavior. How long do you think it will be before society will be allowed to marry multiple partners or you will be asked to attend a religious ceremony where someone marries their dog or cat, or even an imaginary friend? You think I'm joking? In this brave new world we live in, where we can change definitions at will, we must know we are going to encounter a problem—our culture is often operating with a broken moral compass.

This slippery slope has led us to finally descend to the pit of sacrificing babies' lives on the altar of self-centeredness. We are approaching a staggering number. Nearly sixty million babies have been killed through abortion in the United States since the practice was legalized in 1973. Just to give this number some kind of perspective, consider that this is the combined population of twenty-five states in America, plus Washington DC! Just imagine a terrorist wiping out half the states in the USA—what outrage would follow! But our nation considers killing babies a "women's choice" issue. What do you suppose the Giver of Life thinks about our nation's policy of life and death? When He weighs in on the matter, *and He will*...I wonder what that will look like. Even when Planned Parenthood was exposed publicly for heinous crimes of planned mortality for more lucrative sales of aborted babies' body parts, our government continued to support their death mills with our tax dollars.

(Now to be clear, if you are reading this and have had an abortion, God has grace, forgiveness, and restoration for you. These statistics are not intended for your condemnation, but they should be a shocking wake-up call to us as a nation.)

As we continue to examine how nations disregard the self-imposed consequences of their actions, consider recent shifts away from supporting Israel. The United States seems to be leading the way for other nations to consider giving Israel the proverbial cold shoulder. During the Barack Hussein Obama administration years, the White House has increasingly distanced itself from Israel, seeming to give privilege to Israel's enemies. Billions of American tax dollars have flowed into nations committed to destroying Israel. Even John Kerry's negotiated treaty with Iran leaves room for requiring America to defend Iran if Israel is forced to make a preemptive strike against an Iranian nuclear arsenal!

Returning to the proposition of our nation moving toward the tipping point, each of these national changes noted above are flooding more and more compartments of the "USS America." Moral decay, blatant disregard for God's order, pledging allegiance to "self" above the Almighty, backing away from our staunch support of Israel and leaning toward her enemies—all these compartments of our national security are increasingly taking on water. Technology isn't the only sector accelerating at a dizzying pace, so are the ungodly choices of our government and the breakneck speed with which our society is hurling us into a collision course with the God of all creation. Many scoff at the idea of an apocalyptic end to the world as we know it, but they mocked Noah right up until the moment the skies opened up and the water swept them away. Yes, a King is coming, but not as a lamb this time. He is the Lion of the Tribe of Judah, and He is coming to judge the earth; and for many…it won't be a laughing matter.

So if this is where we are in history, what's just around the corner?

The mainstream media has abdicated its role as the watchdog of our society. As a matter of fact, after the 1960s, the public has continually lost more and more trust in the objectivity of the media. It seems that liberal universities and journalists have become strange bedfellows in the influence business and have all but taken over the once "free press." Our Judeo-Christian foundations and social orientation have been replaced by an anti-God bias. Control the information sources, and you can "control," or at least heavily influence, the citizens of a nation. And the enemy of life gloats.

> Yes, a King is coming, but not as a lamb this time. He is the Lion of the Tribe of Judah, and He is coming to judge the earth.

What has begun as honoring small differences, has turned into showing deference, which has turned into political correctness. Inevitably, this progression ends up with the viewpoints of a popular majority being forced to yield to the vantage point of a much smaller sect.

The fringe is now the mainstream, and if you disagree, you had better keep it to yourself. In fact as I write this, a student at Loyola College is defending herself in court for speaking out against the anti-Israel Boycott, Divestment, Sanctions (BDS) policies of the university! Pastors have been prosecuted for "hate speech" crimes for simply quoting the Bible, and students are silenced on college campuses for espousing a "conservative" viewpoint. The so-called tolerant and compassionate left is anything but tolerant or compassionate. In fact, they have been proven to be among the most violent and abusive among us, and are held to very different standards of speech and activism than the rest of society.

A great shaking is coming. As the hull continues to fill with water, one can hear the eerie sounds of the joints and rivets being stressed by the enormous pressure to surrender to the onslaught of the inevitable depths. A Judge is watching. Israel is being abandoned by once faithful allies. People are celebrating their worship of self-absorption and standing by applauding while godless people lead. Dark is becoming darker, and in that darkness, a creeping evil is waiting for the moment to strike. The world is approaching a tipping point and all because...

a King is coming!

Yes, a Lion-Judge is coming. The King who will not be mocked is coming. The apocalyptic signs are abundantly clear. The words from the prophets of old have been appearing in the coverage of modern events in our media. The dot-to-dot picture is now emerging as a clear high definition presentation.

This book is meant to be a warning and yet another wake-up call for those who can still hear and see. It is not a book of political correctness. Many times the truth offends, but that doesn't diminish the veracity or the impact of that truth. Repeatedly in the Scriptures, Yeshua turned to His disciples and asked, "Does this offend you?" Remember this: The point at which you become offended is the point where you will cease to grow, learn, discern, or even understand. Proverbs 18:19 (HCSB) says it like this: *"An offended brother is harder to reach than a fortified city, and quarrels are like the bars of a fortress."*

May truth and understanding explode in our hearts and minds as we see that all signs point to the coming King. This simple truth should change the way we think, pray, give, and live.

CHAPTER 3

The Usurper Who
Would be King

To usurp a throne is to seize it or take it by force through a revolt or coup, with no right or authority to rule. The most infamous revolt of all times took place when the Archangel Lucifer decided he wanted to *sit* on the throne of the Most High instead of *serving* the throne!

The war over *the* throne commenced in heaven because of pride and arrogance, bathed in self-deception. This is the true life story of one of God's most exquisite creations, Lucifer, who was overcome by his own beauty, position of significance, gifting, and pride-filled ambition. I often marvel that a full one-third of the angels of Adonai were deceived by this self-proclaimed king and drank the Kool-Aid of their own eventual destruction. This notorious rebellion is recorded for us by the prophet in Isaiah 14:12-14 (TLV).

How you have fallen from heaven, O brighstar, son of the dawn! How you are cut down to the earth, you who made the nations prostrate! You said in your heart: "I WILL ascend to heaven, I WILL exalt my throne above the stars of God. I WILL sit upon the mount of meeting, in the uttermost parts of the north. I WILL ascend above the high places of the clouds—I WILL make myself like Elyon [the Most High]." (Emphasis mine)

Notice the frequency of a certain pronoun? If you listen carefully when someone speaks, you will learn pretty quickly who, or what, is the center of their affection!

- *"I will* ascend to heaven"—Interesting in that Lucifer was already in the presence of God. I bet he didn't mean he was just going to vacation in heaven, but rather, his intention was to *displace* God in heaven!
- *"I will* exalt my throne above the stars of God"—Lucifer was already over a massive number of stars (angels), but apparently he was not satisfied. He wanted the authority to rule over *all* the angels of God.
- *"I will* sit upon the mount of meeting"—As noted in Isaiah 2:2, Lucifer is not speaking about Mt. Sinai or the Mount of Olives. No, he's saying he will sit enthroned on the Mountain of the Lord!
- *"I will* ascend above the high places of the clouds"—Many times clouds are used to describe the glory of El Olam (God Everlasting) found in the throne room of heaven, and Lucifer is proclaiming that *his* glory would be above the glory of the One who created him!
- *"I will* make myself like Elyon [the Most High]"—Lucifer was declaring that he was going to become the owner of the universe instead of El Elyon (The Most High God). I wonder what his plans might have been for the removal and disposal of the One who has no beginning and no end.

Rebellion always starts in the heart. The soil from which it is birthed is a mix of jealousy and pride, quickly morphing into an unteachable arrogance. This could be likened to the hardening of the heart or the offended brother whose heart becomes like a walled-up city as in Proverbs 18:19. Arrogance breeds a self-righteousness that hungers after supremacy. Rebellion never erupts without being provoked by desires of the heart that crave the satisfaction of self-exaltation.

And there you have the story line of what occurred in God's heaven when Lucifer led the rebellion to usurp the throne of Elohim—the first name of God revealed in Scripture ("In the beginning, Elohim..."), defined by Jewish scholars as Creator and Judge.

At this point in heaven's pre-Adamic history, God said, *"Enough is enough!"* And He cast Satan and one-third of the rebelling angels out of His presence. Jesus said in Luke 10:18, *"I saw Satan fall like lightning from heaven."* So how fast do you think lightning falls from the sky? I would say God "body slammed" Satan out of heaven in the best WWF style ever seen! Bam!

Is there any question as to who was almighty God in that moment? Is it obvious God is Jehovah Sabaoth (The Lord of Hosts)? Is there any doubt who the Creator is and who is the created? The famous singer/songwriter Paul Simon said it best, "I'd rather be a hammer than a nail...yes I would, I surely would."

Consider for a moment a few of the attributes of our God:

- God alone creates life.
- His power is without limit.
- His knowledge and wisdom are unsearchable.
- El Olam (The Everlasting God) has no beginning and no end.
- YHVH (Yahweh, Lord, Jehovah) alone is omnipresent.
- He is the standard of love, goodness, and faithfulness.
- The one true God has never tasted defeat. He fears nothing or no one.
- Our heavenly Father knows the future as completely as the past.
- He alone is never taken by surprise.

Satan is so deceived that even today he is still at war with God, still trying to usurp the throne of Messiah—Jesus, the soon-coming King! Much of what we are observing in the events of our day is the foreshadowing of Jesus' second coming and the final judgment of mankind...along with all the fallen angels.

But the story continues, and the war escalates in the garden of Eden, where God created mankind. In the garden we find the rebellious one, who was cast down to Earth, spinning a lie to deceive the crown of God's new creation—mankind.

> *Now the serpent was more crafty than any of the wild animals the Lord God had made. He said to the woman, "Did God really say, 'You must not eat from any tree in the garden'?"*
>
> *The woman said to the serpent, "We may eat fruit from the trees in the garden, but God did say, 'You must not eat fruit from the tree that is in the middle of the garden, and you must not touch it, or you will die.'"*
>
> *"You will not certainly die," the serpent said to the woman. "For God knows that when you eat from it your eyes will be opened, and you will be like God, knowing good and evil."* (Genesis 3:1-5)

Think about what Satan did to Eve in the garden and then to Adam as well. Is there a pattern you recognize in the conversation above? First, he brings into question what God said. He starts with the truth, and then he slightly twists it, which brings confusion as to what exactly was said in the first place! Truth mixed with the smallest amount of error is no longer truth. Next Satan tries to get her slightly off balance with twists to the truth, sprinkled with question marks. Can you imagine what Eve was going through? "Huh...no God didn't say we couldn't eat from all the trees. But wait a second, He did say not to eat from the one tree in the middle of the garden because there would be severe consequences if we did eat from that one." Then the enemy states that God is a liar and backs up that bold statement with a convincing argument concerning God's motive for withholding something good from Eve.

Satan lies about God, about circumstances, and then about the future, in order to get us to believe him instead of God. Everything goes south from there. The devil's own self-deception is so complete, and his DNA is so permanently stained, that his very name was changed to *The Father of Lies*!

And with the lie, Satan convinced Eve to rebel. He dangled the carrot of desire for something greater than God initially offered her— or so she thought. The goodness of God was now in question. Could God be trusted for her happiness and fulfillment? Is our God like some alley cat who amuses Himself with a half-dead mouse, only to kill and destroy it in the end?

Could a contract with the devil be more valuable than a covenant with Jehovah? Could the word of a deceiver be more reliable than the promise of the living God? The simple answer to these questions may seem obvious to you reading these words, but the practical working out of discerning the manipulation of the moment may be quite another task. Debating and second-guessing is a major tactic Satan uses to deceive mankind as he seeks to replace the rightful King of Glory. Please don't forget, this is the ultimate *war for the throne*, and the grand prize…is *you*!

Unfortunately, his debating prowess has won him some major successes in his multi-pronged strategies to become the god of this world. Consider, for instance, the 1.1 billion deceived people on Earth who follow the teachings of Muhammad and Islam. Or, imagine the 1.2 billion walking in Hinduism or the five hundred million who declare Buddha to be their god. And let's not forget the massive number of people currently being misled by the New Age movement, as secular humanism (life without God) has truly become one of America's "religions" of choice.

Usurpers of thrones are not exclusive to Satan's many attempts to displace Adonai, but they are strangely related. He has worked long and hard in every generation to cut off the promises of Jehovah and break the royal bloodline of authority. For instance, take the conspiracy of King David's son Absalom to usurp his father's throne in 2 Samuel, chapter 15. Although David had mercy on Absalom's transgressions, the young man's desire for the top spot in the kingdom could not be quenched. Through lies, deceit, and the help of many powerful men, Absalom bullied his way to the throne, displacing the father who loved him. Absalom and his army pursued David after he fled the palace, having it in his heart to eliminate David from the scene. But Absalom was later killed in combat, his army was destroyed, and David returned to the throne. El Olam, the Righteous Judge, sees everything from His throne, and He watches over His promises to perform them (Jeremiah 1:12).

Usually a usurper has no respect for law and order, the rule of authority, or the Word of God. When a man or an entire people rebel against the throne over all thrones, the results will always be disastrous. The history of ancient Israel from the time of Moses forward is simply rife with too many examples to highlight here.

Later in King David's life, we see yet another son usurper at work, trying to take what is not rightfully his. Adonijah, David's fourth son, saw the death of his two older brothers and considered himself the heir-apparent to the throne. He proclaimed himself king, while apparently forgetting to send an invitation to his father, King David, and his brother Solomon. *Oops*!

Solomon's mother, Queen Bathsheba, and Nathan the Prophet quickly met with King David, explained the coup, and orders were given for Solomon to be crowned the rightful king of Israel. God gave wisdom to both David and Solomon to re-secure not only the throne, but the bloodline of Yeshua the Messiah.

Men can try to usurp kingdoms, Satan can try to usurp God's throne, and even nations can try to usurp God's standards and rule over the earth. When a nation takes a stand against the clear counsel of God, that nation is just begging to be judged, and eventually it will be.

I continue to wonder, at what point is it that God has had enough when a nation tries to ignore His clearly expressed standards? Does the patience of God Himself have a *tipping point*? Consider Genesis 6:3, if you will. *"Then the Lord said, 'My Spirit will not contend with humans forever, for they are mortal; their days will be a hundred and twenty years.'"* But God is patient, you say, and God is love. Yes, without a doubt; and His justice, righteousness, and truth will have the last word, every time!

> When a nation takes a stand against the clear counsel of God, that nation is just begging to be judged, and eventually it will be.

Make no mistake, the signs are all around us, and they are all pointing to one glorious event—the coming of a King! Sound the trumpet to the sleeping Church. Awake to clarity expressed in Scripture! Clean your spiritual glasses so you can see and your spiritual ears so you can hear. The Lord of all desires that each of us gain His perspective, so we can participate and prepare for His Kingdom to come in great power. This world will be altered in a significant way, and we must be prepared for the fulfillment of these historic events.

We can live in the deception broadcast by the Liar and passively walk in the misconception that everything will be as it always has been. Or, we can invite the clarity of the Lamp of the Light of the World into our discovery process and join God in what He is doing in this period in which we live.

It is absolutely critical that we keep this one truth as the primary filter through which we make decisions and choices in life. And that truth is that Jehovah, the God of Abraham, Isaac, and Jacob is the only true and living God; and that His Son, Yeshua, Jesus Christ, is the only Savior, our Messiah and King Redeemer. The Bible is the Word of the living God, true and accurate. Its message of the gospel of Christ has the power to save the lost, heal the sick, and bring wisdom and revelation. This God truly is the creator and sustainer of our daily life. We must understand that He will not be mocked forever. Let us not presume upon His mercy, but responsibly act according to what we say we believe, being *doers* of His word and not merely hearers! He has called us to be disciples, not spectators, because these *are* the days of Elijah!

Shake off the predictable drone of the mainstream media and the Hollywood elites' appeal for social correctness, and let's get back to the good old-fashioned truth of the Bible. What do you say? The signs are all around us.

So wake up! The usurper of the throne will not have his way. Yeshua will prevail, and He will have His throne because He *is*…

the King who is coming!

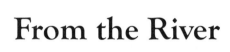

CHAPTER 4

From the River
to the Sea...

D
o you know the rest of the Palestinian chant I quoted above? It goes like this: "From the river to the sea, Palestine will soon be free." Who are these people, what river and what sea are they shouting about, and where is Palestine, you may ask? All good questions. The river sung about in this little rhyme is the Jordan River, which separates Israel and the nation of Jordan from each other. It connects the Sea of Galilee in the north to the Dead Sea in the south. The sea mentioned is the Mediterranean Sea, which forms a natural border for Israel on its entire west coast. And where is Palestine? Well, the enemies of Israel, the Palestinians, claim that all the lands included in their little chant are the *historic homeland* of the Palestinian people, vis-à-vis, Israel.

One small problem with their claims: There has *never* been a nation of Arabs known as Palestine, and the "Palestinian people" are a relatively new invention of the terrorist turned diplomat and... Nobel Peace Prize winner, Yasser Arafat of the Palestine Liberation Organization in the 1970s.

These enemies of Israel say the key to peace in the Middle East is to destroy the modern State of Israel and wipe the Jewish people off the face of the earth! Pretty radical solution, don't you think? But this just proves there is nothing new under the sun, as King Solomon said so many years ago. This genocidal pattern has deep roots in the history of mankind—the Pharaoh of the Exodus (Exodus 1:16), Haman of Persia (Esther 3:6), King Herod (Matthew 2:16), the Spanish Inquisition of the late 1400s, the Russian Pogroms of the nineteenth century, the Nazi Holocaust of WWII, the Islamic Jihad of modern times, and ultimately the Great Tribulation of the end of times (Ezekiel 38-39; Zechariah 13-14).

In the past, Christians may have taken a kind of laissez-faire attitude toward the situation, but as of late, the battle cry of the radical Muslim Jihadist has changed to include Christians as well. "First the Saturday people, then the Sunday people" (meaning, "Kill the Jews, then the Christians") is the battle cry that has been heard more than once in the past several decades. And they have been good to their word as the Islamic State of Iraq and Syria (ISIS) continues to slaughter entire Christian communities in the Middle East. In fact, experts say that the ancient Christian communities in the Middle East may be completely wiped out by the year 2020…only three years from the publishing of this book!

"But *why us*? What have we done to these people?" some Christians might ask. First of all, when it comes to radical Islam, you don't have to do anything to deserve death (in their eyes). If you are not one of them, you are fodder for the grave. An infidel, from their perspective, is anyone who does not worship their god, in their way, with their understanding, and infidels deserve death. They would also say that Christianity is not pure monotheism because Christians worship God as revealed in three personalities—Father, Son, and Holy Spirit. This also makes for an infidel, according to Islamic beliefs. Also, consider in the Bible, the apostle Paul teaches that Christians have been included in the "commonwealth of Israel" and worship Yeshua (Jesus of Nazareth), the King of the Jews! Did you know there is an inscription in Arabic around the Dome of the Rock mosque on the Temple Mount that reads, "There is no god but Allah, and he has no son." So if you are a Christian, that's one of the main reasons why *you* are on their radar.

To explain this further, let me take you back a few hundred years in time to the Babylonian captivity. The person of interest is the young prophet Zechariah who, along with his grandfather, Iddo, has been released to return to their beloved homeland, Israel. His writings are dated somewhere around 520-518 BC, and it was a good time to be an Israelite again. The prophet Haggai is instructing the people to rebuild the House of the Lord, and Zerubbabel is the governor of Judah. Israel is returning from seventy years of captivity in Babylon (Iraq), and things are starting to look up. The cities are being rebuilt, flocks and herds are multiplying, grain will be harvested in season, and vines are starting to produce their fruit again. Nehemiah is building the walls to protect the holy city, and Ezra is instructing the people from the Torah. It seems as though everything is back on track. Joshua is the High Priest, and Israel is turning back to the God of their fathers Abraham, Isaac, and Jacob. All quiet on the Eastern front? Well, not so fast! Remember, this is the real war for a throne, and the usurper is still up to his old tricks.

Just a few generations later, we pick up the battle in a distant land called Persia, which is called Iran today. The king's name is Ahasuerus, or Xerxes, and he rules from India to Ethiopia from his royal throne in the citadel of Susa. His kingdom is made up of 127 provinces and many people groups and cultures...including all the Jews. Mordecai, a Jew descended from the captives of Jerusalem taken by Nebuchadnezzar of Babylon, lived in Susa and adopted his cousin Esther (Hadassah) when her parents died. She is an orphan who is adopted and grafted into Mordecai's family. She is Jewish, but she hides her roots and takes a Persian name. She lives outside of Israel, grows in beauty and wisdom, marries the king of the entire known world, and resides in the palace with grace and influence.

Now, the way that Esther becomes the queen is interesting, too. As it happens, the king needs a new queen because the former one (Queen Vashti) lost her head, and Esther (the Jewish girl) is selected for the position. At the same time, a nobleman by the name of Haman was elevated to the highest position in the kingdom, second only to the king himself. That's cool, right? What's wrong with that? Nothing, except that the pesky Jew Mordecai, Esther's uncle, won't bow down and give Haman the honor that he craves and demands.

You know the story from here, don't you? Haman is beside himself with anger and rage, and instead of dealing with Mordecai as a single problem, he decides that *all* the Jews are a rebellious race and should be wiped off the face of the earth! What in the world could bring a sane human being to such a conclusion? And not only that, but Haman also succeeds in convincing the king to eliminate all the Jews in the kingdom. Amazing! Just keep in mind that there is a throne at stake here; it's not one that you can see with your naked eye, but a real throne, nonetheless.

There is also a little known fact in play that you could miss if you were speed-reading the text. Haman's full name should cause us to pause for just a second and scratch our heads. He is Haman son of Hammedatha, the Agagite. Agagite...what's an Agagite? (Sounds like a species of rock from sixth grade science class to me.) It means he is a descendant of King Agag of the Amalekites, whom Adonai instructed King Saul of Israel to destroy completely. But King Saul didn't do it, and it cost him his throne, his sanity, and eventually his life. Do you think Haman knew Mordecai's family history? I do, and when Haman also discovered that Mordecai was a Jew...well, the war of thrones continued! It is also interesting to me that Zechariah prophesies a King for Jerusalem in the ninth chapter of his book, which further exacerbates the situation and gives us all a huge clue as to *why* Jerusalem is being restored in the first place. (Hint: For the answer to the clue mentioned here, refer once again to the title of the book.)

Now back to our story. We are confronted here with a very big problem. A King is coming to a certain people and a certain place at a certain time. The only trouble now is that those certain people are about to be wiped off the face of the earth! *No problem*! I want to make a declaration here you can take to the bank: When Jehovah makes a promise, a covenant, a pledge, *He will see it through to completion.* Remember, when you run up against a road block, a deal breaker, or some such thing, rest assured as my friend Don Moen sang…"God will make a way where there seems to be no way." God always has the answer!

So what was the answer in this situation? God had a young Jewish girl hidden in the palace right under the king's nose (and Haman's). When the time was right, Esther fasted and prayed, the God of the Jews gave her a plan, she revealed Haman's treachery, the bad guy and all his sons (a very important part of the story, often overlooked) were hanged on a scaffold one hundred feet

> When Jehovah makes a promise, a covenant, a pledge, *He will see it through to completion.*

high, and the Jews were saved. Why? Come on, let's say it together… *because a King is coming!*

Can you see that the ultimate purpose for getting rid of the Jews is because a King is coming *through* them and *for* them? So if the enemy of Jehovah can do away with God's plan of redemption by wiping out the vessel (Israel), which carries the new wineskin and the new wine (which is the New Covenant and the Holy Spirit), then Israel and the nations will be left with no hope of salvation! And can you further see that all the conflicts against the sons of Jacob through time have indeed been this unseen war for the throne?

If you are starting to see my point, then maybe, just maybe, there is a chance that we can impact the world's opinion of Israel, the Jewish people, and get a full-fledged *"anti*-anti-Semitism" campaign going that will have some teeth in it!

Before I continue my rant here, let me remind you that according to Scripture, the Holy Bible, the blessing of Abram *and his seed* is the key to the blessing of *all* the nations and peoples on Earth. What, you've never seen that before? Well listen to the words of almighty God from His conversation with Abram (later called Abraham) in Genesis, chapter 12.

> *My heart's desire is to make you into a great nation, to bless you, to make your name great so that you may be a*

blessing. My desire is to bless those who bless you, but whoever curses you I will curse, and in you ALL the families of the earth will be blessed. (Genesis 12: 2-3 TLV, emphasis mine)

Did you catch the short word in small caps in the text above? You see, that little word "all" includes *you*! You are a part of the "all peoples on earth" that God is speaking to Abram about. And if you will bless the Jewish people, the promise of a blessing from heaven also belongs to you. Can you see how the devil has tried to make the Jewish people the enemy of mankind for all these millennia, when the truth is that they are the instrument of God for the blessing and salvation of all mankind! It makes perfect sense, then, that the devil would also paint the salvation of Israel as her worst enemy, namely Yeshua HaMashiach, Jesus Christ, Israel's Messiah. Come on somebody! Can I get a really good *Amen* from the balcony? This is exactly why we have anti-Semitism, the BDS movement, Neo-Nazism, ISIS, terrorism, and on and on. *If the enemy can get the world to reject the packaging, then the world will also miss the blessing.*

Now let me bring this Esther narrative into the twenty-first century. Today, as in the time of Zechariah, Nehemiah, and all the other "iah's," Israel is being gathered back to her ancient homeland on the Mediterranean. They are coming in great numbers from Europe, the former Soviet Union, Latin America, North America, China, Ethiopia, indeed from every nation where He scattered them (Ezekiel 36:24; Jeremiah 30:3). He is gathering His children back home. The crops are planted, the flocks and herds are multiplying, the grapes are ripening on the vines, the prophets are crying out in the streets, and the songs of Zion are being sung in the land. And just as in the time of the first re-gathering from Babylon, there is another Persian (Iran) who is crying out for the extermination of *all* the Jews, the elimination of the "Zionist entity," as they say. "Wipe Israel off the face of the earth, kill the Jews, for they are the source of all our troubles and wars," they scream. These voices are not some mysterious hidden face behind an Internet blog. No, these are world leaders, presidents, and premiers. They are allowed an international platform on the stages of the United Nations building in New York City and podiums in our finest institutions of higher education! Yes, the spirit of Haman is alive and well today. He is even occupying the same seat that he did during the days of Esther and Mordecai.

Ah, but not to fear...the God of the Jews has a plan! He always has a plan because He knows the beginning from the end. This is the huge advantage we have over the adversary of our souls. So what's the plan?

Like in the time of Esther, God has a Jewish girl hidden in the palace! She was born a Jew, then adopted and grafted into the commonwealth of Israel. She lived in every foreign land, hid her Jewish identity, took a Gentile name, and followed the celebrations of the nations where she lived. She grew in beauty and majesty, and she's married to *the* King. Do you know her name? That's right—*the Church* is her name.

> Like in the time of Esther, God has a Jewish girl hidden in the palace—*the Church* is her name.

And now that the plot to destroy all the Jews has been revealed... her uncle, Mordecai (Messianic Jews), is begging her (the Church) to go before the King and intercede for the lives of her relatives. But will she do it? Will she fast and pray? Will she cry out as a watchman on the walls? Or will she remain silent, hoping the curse will somehow disappear, saying, "I am not of those people any longer; they rejected their King and I am married to Him; they brought these troubles on their own heads; why should I stick my neck out for them? If they are God's chosen people, then He will certainly take care of them!"

Listen to the words of Mordecai when Hadassah, Esther was concerned for her own safety above the salvation of her people.

Do not think that because you are in the king's house you alone of all the Jews will escape. For if you remain silent at this time, relief and deliverance for the Jews will arise from

another place, but you and your father's family will perish.
And who knows but that you have come to royal position
for such a time as this? (Esther 4:12-14)

Yes, that's right, Church! You are God's hidden plan for the salvation of Israel and the blessing of all the peoples on Earth! Will you fast and pray? Will you go before the King and cry out for your people? Or will you continue to give comfort and aid to Haman, embrace replacement theology (discussed in chapter 8), support BDS, and refuse shelter and supply to the Jews? For if you remain silent at this time, relief and deliverance for the Jews will arise from another place, but you will have missed the day of your visitation—even the very purpose for which you were brought to the Kingdom. The adversary, the usurper, is seeking to destroy the whole house of Israel again because...

a King is coming!

CHAPTER 5

Changing Values:
Political Correctness vs.
Biblical Correctness

BaBoom! Can you hear the clash of competing values in society today? I know you are certainly feeling the effects of these massive shifts in your daily life. Values you have historically held in high regard have now been slammed up against new morphing standards, resulting in the formation of huge dividing lines within our nation and world. It seems as if no one is at the wheel of this behemoth as it heads downhill at an ever-increasing velocity, intent on destroying itself along with everything in its self-centered path.

Instead of America the Beautiful, a nation known for our unity and generosity, we have become known as a people who are terribly divided, angry, and intolerant of each other. Instead of our great diversity bringing us rich blessings, we have allowed battle lines to form within our nation on any front you might imagine—race, gender, religion, politics, ethics, economics. You name it, and we have a smoldering wick ready to burst into flames at any small or even imagined provocation. And it gets worse! We have a new label for those who wish to speak out against this insanity. We now call them intolerant, racists, bigots, homophobes, and purveyors of hate speech. There are even those who declare the Bible, the Word of God, to be the worst kind of hate speech and that it should be banned from our public and private discourse! We don't discuss or debate differences and come to a resolution any longer. Instead, we rub metal on unyielding metal, and the resulting sound is a national house divided.

Have you noticed that a democratic society rarely retains its original founding values? In fact, I have read that the normal life span for a democracy is between two hundred and three hundred years. The constant shifting of internal and external forces contributes to this change in both people and nations. Societies evolve. In certain ways they progress, while others may regress, or even just dissolve.

During the last 240 years, we have seen some incredible advances in medicine, transportation, communication, and civil liberties. Did you know that life expectancy in the first century was only about thirty years? However, the life expectancy for both males and females in the United States today is well into the eighties. There was a period of time in this nation when women were not allowed to vote. There was an era when many sicknesses and diseases led to certain death. I grew up in the days when there were still "Whites Only" restrooms, drinking fountains, and restaurants. Valuable goods could not always be easily transported, and critical communication used to seemingly take forever to reach the intended recipient. All this and more has changed so radically that it is almost impossible to keep up with the latest trends and gadgets that form and transform our society.

I saw an article recently in one of my motorcycle magazines that was celebrating the one-hundred-year anniversary of the first cross-continental motorcycle run—by two women! The year was 1916, and two sisters mounted a pair of Indian Motorcycles on Long Island for a cross-country, never-been-done-before-by-anyone, motor adventure. They did run into a small cultural snag just outside Chicago, Illinois, of all places, when they were arrested for wearing men's motorcycle clothing! Can you imagine anything like this happening today? They were later released, because they were wearing the only motorcycle protective clothing that was available in those days, which was made only for men! It's unbelievable how our culture has changed. I can even remember back in the late fifties seeing photographs of women in bathing suits on public beaches who were being measured by police officers for the proper skirt length. Am I that old? Former Olympian, now transgender, Bruce Caitlyn Jenner wouldn't have even made it to the parking lot in those days!

Also noteworthy, since the founding and establishing of the United States, we have embraced Judeo-Christian beliefs above any other religious system or values. Since the very beginning, our society valued life in the womb as the law and norm of acceptance in our nation. Now, backed by the courts, we have redefined life in the womb to coincide with our society's desire to determine whether a new life is convenient or inconvenient for an individual and, therefore, free to be destroyed. Religious and life values, in general, have taken a crazy downturn...with resulting consequences, I might add.

Now some of these values are caught, but many of them are taught as well. I remember very clearly the year 1958. We had moved from Waterville, Maine, to Derry, New Hampshire. I was seven years old, and I walked to school with my sister who was in first grade. The old brick two-room schoolhouse was just a few hundred yards from our small home. Grades one to three were in one room, and across the hall were the "big" kids in fourth through sixth grades. Our two rooms were separated by a big pot-bellied stove, which, along with the oil furnace in the basement, would keep us toasty warm during the long New England winters. Every day would start the same way, right on time, no exceptions ever. As the clock struck 8:30 a.m., we were all assembled in our seats for homeroom activities and instructions. To start the day, the teacher would stand at her desk, open a Bible, and read to us from the Scriptures. Next, we would all bow our heads, close our eyes, and repeat the Lord's Prayer. Lastly, we all stood at attention beside our desks, placed our hand over our heart, and recited the Pledge of Allegiance. No one would have dreamt of opting out of these early morning exercises or protesting the legality of *all* participating, no matter what your religious affiliation might be. The Bible, the God of Abraham, and the American flag were all symbols that united us and defined us as a people—no questions asked!

For most of our nation's history, we financially rewarded those who excelled in business, industry, and education. Now, we value and financially reward those in the entertainment industry, athletics, and software companies that keep us occupied, entertained, and productive. Does this say something about our priorities and passions as a society?

Since the beginning of time, marriage was defined as the union between a man and a woman. Now households have been turned upside down; marriage has been redefined as the union between two consenting adults, no matter their gender—natural or altered. What's next? Don't be shocked to see animal rights folks wanting to "marry" their pets or astrologists marrying asteroids and stars. When you begin to re-define the terms, who's to say where it should stop? When the Word of our Creator is shunned for the thoughts of men, we are on a slippery slope that does not promise a good end result.

The greatest value of our nation is no longer its growth and unity as a whole, but rather, the self-centered desires of each individual. We even disrespect and dishonor serving the family unit as a whole, replacing it with the value of serving oneself. Abortion *rights* are a perfect example of this. Abortion itself is against all traditional family concepts—killing the baby for convenience sake. It affects both the father and the mother and causes a breakdown in the entire family structure as God has designed it. And we continue to vote for politicians who promise more of the same—more money for the abortion factories, more death, more misery, and all in, *supposedly*, in the name of "compassion" and women's "rights." Truly our national conscience has been seared to the point that we are no longer confronted by our own sin. Can anyone see a tipping point here?

> The greatest value of our nation is no longer its growth and unity as a whole, but rather, the self-centered desires of each individual.

This list of shifting values in our nation goes on and on, but suffice it to say, our country is more concerned with transforming individual desires above preserving or building upon bedrock principles. As Christians and Jews passively sat by, God was being displaced through a well-planned and executed strategy from secular humanists. The educational system became the delivery vehicle of the slow-acting, numbing poison that progressively eradicated God's standards from our society. A *perfect storm* erupted when the courts jumped in, usurping Congressional power by "writing law." And the electorate within God's Church submissively watched their precious country, and freedoms, being overthrown.

In 1954, then-Senator (later Vice President, then President) Lyndon Baines Johnson wrote a piece of legislation, the Johnson Amendment, which would go a long way to silence the churches and synagogues who were not yet asleep at the switch. He would threaten the clergy with a response from the Internal Revenue Service if they were to take up social and political issues from their pulpits. This law, or threat, still stands today, and anyone holding a 501(c)(3) tax-exempt status with the United States government knows that it has teeth that will bite hard should you test its veracity. The action taken by LBJ has effectively removed the voice of righteousness from the marketplace, and essentially it enables government to operate without a conscience.

Are you politically correct?

Once we excommunicated the God of Abraham and His pesky standards of living—the Bible—the next item on the agenda has become raising the banner of our latest man-made god...*political correctness*. Biblical correctness has now been shoved aside by our government, educators, businesses, entertainment industry, liberal media, and wealthy social elites. With such a vast array of worshipers, this god we will call PC (for convenience sake), has become the one who could change any law that did not support the secular humanist's alter-constitution. Because we have become a nation consumed with self, we now have gay marriage, open borders, extended "rights" of radical Islamic invaders, forced national funding of abortion, pastors prosecuted for hate speech…and the list goes on and on.

The so-called Liberals and Progressives have pulled down the altar of God and erected a new altar to the god of political correctness. As in the day of Daniel, all must bow to this image or risk being thrown in the fiery furnace of public opinion. The god of PC promotes a woman's choice to kill her unborn child if that life is an inconvenience, and it authorizes the sale of aborted baby body parts in the name of medical advancement. Pornography on television, movies, Internet, social media, and gaming, accelerates the agenda of political correctness. PC promotes itself with an air of educated snobbery and an aloof pride of sensitivity towards the downtrodden. But don't be fooled! Behind that soft and understanding façade lies a vicious foe with a wounded soul, and he will do anything to protect the position he has fought so long and hard to acquire.

Perhaps I should pause here and give you the definition of political correctness from *Wikipedia*.

> Political correctness, commonly abbreviated to PC, is a term which, in modern usage, is used to describe language, policies, or measures which are intended not to offend or disadvantage any particular group of people in society.

The *Huffington Post* noted in June of 2016, that insistence on political correctness can create real problems and go too far.

> In stifling speech, it can make important topics off limits to reasonable study and discussion. It can encourage harassment of those who are viewed as not politically correct, in short using one form of intolerance to try to prevent another. Political correctness can excuse and thus prevent people from fully developing the ability to defend their views, to defeat weak thinking with sound argument. And, in extreme cases, especially in less democratic

societies than our own, political correctness can be used by leaders to suppress freedom on the false justification that they are "protecting" others.

In our educational system, we have seen teachers reprimanded for talking about intelligent design, and students who wore crosses were ordered to take them off because someone could be offended. Even our military chaplains are told what they can and cannot do or say. Many of our historical buildings and books are being altered to erase references to Scripture or the God of the Bible. Beyond being initially marginalized, Jews and Christians are being viewed as second-class citizens and somehow put on par with hate groups.

Even within our governmental structure, political correctness is not only running rampant, but it's also putting citizens' safety at risk. Retired General Michael Haden, appearing on CNN in June 2016, said there was a hesitance to pursue some cases for fear of being branded a bigot. The former director of the CIA and NSA has noted that the U.S. Army may have backed off the Fort Hood terrorist, radical Muslim Nidal Hasan, due to political correctness issues.

Real justice weighs two different arguments, rightly revealing the true weight of both sides. We see great differences within our justice system, our business communities, and the lifestyles in our nation. We learn to show tolerance for different people and ideas, even if those differences only represent a very small percentage of the people. But tolerance, by definition, does not require the total restructuring of laws, societal norms, and certainly not a restructuring of God's standards, which He established at creation.

Political correctness is not concerned with right or wrong when addressing issues or groups. It does not hold to any historical or biblical anchor, nor is it guided by any type of moral or ethical compass. In fact, in the name of political correctness, what used to be labeled a sin by society (and certainly by God) has now been "cleansed" and redefined through the doctrine of inclusiveness. A wrong is now declared right if a majority of people (or those sitting in positions of authority) declare it not to be wrong. Through the PC relabeling by our society (media, entertainment, government, educational communities, etc.), evil—as defined by God—is now declared both acceptable and protected by our newly revised laws.

Fine and dandy…but there *is* a problem!

God's standard is unchanged and He *is* concerned with right and wrong. The Bible notes in Isaiah 50:20, *"Woe to those who call evil good and good evil; who put darkness for light, and light for darkness; who put bitter for sweet, and sweet for bitter!"* And Proverbs 16:25 (NASB), written by the wisest man who ever lived, declares, *"There is a way which seems right to a man, but its end is the way of death."*

Humanity is consumed with what is best for it—*right now*. It is shortsighted and focused on immediate gratification. Our society's current behavior requires a change in our moral code, not the other way around, as it *should* be. No longer are there absolutes—it is all relative and continually morphing. Again, *self* is king, and any evil can be rationalized to become our new norm of acceptability.

And where do we find the Church at large on this debate between political correctness and biblical correctness? Basically, silent.

It seems to me that many of "God's people" are more concerned about offending others than they are about offending God Himself!

Perhaps some are fearful to speak up, afraid of the harsh intolerance. Maybe others are confused over the seemingly "fair and logical" arguments of society. I have a hunch that most have not defined their clear convictions, which should be gained out of allegiance to God's infallible Word. Many have bought into the lie, prompted by Satan, that God didn't really mean what He clearly said in Scripture, and a new interpretation is more acceptable to them in today's modern and enlightened world.

Yes, there are absolutes in this world which cannot be altered by time, opinion, or preferences. In Deuteronomy 6:4 we read these words, handed down to us through Moses: *"Sh'ma Yisrael, Adonai Eloheinu, Adonai echad!"* Translated: *"Hear O Israel, the Lord our God, the Lord alone."* Yeshua, Jesus said in John 14:6: *"I am the way, the truth and the life. No one comes to the Father except through me."* By these statements, He excluded all other competing well-intentioned religions or philosophies. God made only one provision for reconciling humanity to Himself.

From creation until now, and into every tomorrow, God wants all people to choose His clearly revealed standards over society's *changing lusts*. You have a free will, but make no mistake about it— you are choosing by your actions or failure to act. God is not looking for us to integrate the world's way into His standards, nor is He looking to "relevantly" integrate His declarations into what society desires at the moment. We are not supposed to be "adding God" into the plans that *we've* already decided upon. Rather, we are to bring our lives into conformity with *His* commandments, plans, and purposes for us. He is looking for us to adjust what we are doing, filtered by His Word, and live according to His biblical correctness. *"For my thoughts are not your thoughts, neither are your ways my ways,' declares the Lord. 'As the heavens are higher than the earth, so are my ways higher than your ways and my thoughts than your thoughts'"* (Isaiah 55:8-9).

We don't process things like God does. Are you shocked? His knowledge of the future is without error. Yet somehow we— individually, as a church, or even as a nation—consider our collective mental abilities to be of greater reliability than what God clearly lays out in His Word. Now, we may not blatantly say that, but our lives and decisions indicate the validity of that statement. His Word, the Bible, is correct and more reliable than the politically correct viewpoints of our society, which continues in flux. God doesn't change, nor does His Word change (Malachi 3:6).

Here are the bad-news, good-news statements:

Bad news: If we live according to society's politically correct and shifting standards, we jeopardize our ability to connect with almighty God and hear His leadership. If we filter life's decisions through the strainer of political correctness, then we are lifting that standard above biblical correctness. In other words, we choose to offend God and His standard, rather than risk offending other people.

Good news: If we live according to God's biblically-revealed standards, we receive His favor, protection, grace, provision, and the smile of His presence. Those requiring allegiance to political correctness will undoubtedly resist us strongly…but I would ask yet another question of you: Is it better to please God or man?

Believers in the God of Abraham, Isaac, and Jacob, and in His Son-Messiah, were never called to operate as a subculture in any land, simply fitting into the warp and woof of society. (In weaving, the "warp" are the threads that run lengthwise and the "woof" are the threads that run across the loom making up the foundation of the fabric.) But, rather, we were created to be a counterculture in every nation, to call the people to righteousness and faith in the One True God. And, ideally, the same guiding lamp and light of the scriptures would then become the underpinnings of the entire nation we inhabit.

> If we filter life's decisions through the strainer of political correctness, then we are lifting that standard above biblical correctness.

"Oh come on Paul, now you're dreaming!" Well, then, don't wake me up! What about Babylon (Iraq) under Daniel and his three companions, or Egypt coming under the rulership of Joseph, or Persia enjoying the grace of God with Mordecai and Esther? And…how about our own United States of America, whose Constitution and Declaration of Independence were fashioned after the book of Deuteronomy? Can you see now why our founding documents come under such attack and scrutiny from the radical left? Same spirit as in ancient times, just different names and organizations!

Therefore, I boldly proclaim wherever I find myself in this world, "I am *not* ashamed of the gospel of Messiah, and I am *not* afraid of man; what can man do to me?"

We looked at Wikipedia's definition of political correctness a few pages ago. But the apostle Paul brings clarity to the process of evaluating life's choices from God's perspective as well. He notes that when we make decisions solely from man's perspective, we are limited, unlikely to experience the real truth, and literally setting ourselves up *against* God. Listen to the words of one of the most learned and successful men of the first century, speaking about political correctness and biblical correctness—way ahead of the curve.

> *Those who live according to the flesh have their minds set on what the flesh desires; but those who live in accordance with the Spirit have their minds set on what the Spirit desires. The mind governed by the flesh is death, but the mind governed by the Spirit is life and peace. The mind governed by the flesh is hostile to God; it does not submit to God's law, nor can it do so. Those who are in the realm of the flesh cannot please God.* (Romans 8:5-8)

The first thing to note from this passage is that man's perspective, many times, is fatally limited by his desires, lusts, and the things he treasures. Therefore, the glass through which he views life is filtered, or even obscured, by how he feels, what he perceives to be the truth, or what he experiences. But when a person yields his soul (mind, will, and emotions) to the leadership of the Spirit of God, then that person's life and ambitions are invigorated by God's amazing power and understanding! I want that; what about you?

The apostle Paul then drops a bomb when he said that if a person's mind is governed and influenced only by the natural realm, that person is actually viewed as hostile to God, unable to submit to God's standards. Further, the writer of two-thirds of the New Testament says the person relying solely on his own desires has no hope or ability to please God. Zip. Zero. Nada! Wow, pretty important stuff!

So now it's decision time: Live by reliance on our mind, emotions, other people's standards and opinions, or live by God's Word and His Spirit. Do we choose to make decisions based upon what is politically correct or biblically correct? Bob Dylan wrote a famous line years ago after making a commitment to Jesus as his personal Messiah. He really nailed this thing on the head with his timeless song, "Serve

Somebody." He wrote, "...now it might be the devil, and it might be the Lord, but you're gonna have to serve somebody." We can't have it both ways. We *will* offend someone, but the only question remaining is: Who will it be?

Perhaps Joshua of old said it best; *"If it seems bad to you to worship ADONAI, then choose for yourselves today whom you will serve—whether the gods that your fathers worshipped that were beyond the River or the gods of the Amorites in whose land you are living. But as for me and my household, we will worship ADONAI!"* (Joshua 24:15 TLV). You can't put off the decision forever because...

a King is coming!

CHAPTER 6

Will the Real Church
Please Wake Up?

Have you experienced times of being overwhelmed with the various pulls on your life? Maybe all the juggling of priorities, tasks, and responsibilities becomes so intense that you feel you are going to drop something important. You rise early, and the demands of the day immediately start calling your name. And they don't stop, even when you crash at night, falling onto your pillow. Well, news flash: *You are not alone!*

We're all tired—mentally, emotionally, physically, and even spiritually. Tomorrow is likely to be a repeat of today. Soon you feel as though you are walking around in some type of fog, unable to distinguish one moment from the next. You wonder, how in the world do I get off this roller coaster and get back to living the kind of life God created me to live?

In today's modern society, where technology speaks to you every moment from your computer, cell phone, and now even from your "smart" watch, you are being asked to do more with less time or resources. Multi-taskers have become the new superheroes, and those of us without this sought-after, super-gifting fall in the wake of the progress of others. Both opportunities and challenges mount up, while reminders regarding your core priorities and values scream at you to pay up. Then, it seems like more "good opportunities" keep you from completing your top priorities, while more voices call for your attention—no, they *demand* your attention! "Of course I can multi-task," you assure yourself, while sinking deeper and deeper into the mire of unresolved problems and incomplete tasks.

You didn't plan to be caught up in this state of settle-for sub-normalcy, but here you are. It seems that the priorities you said were important don't seem to make it to the top of your list to receive your full attention. You start the downward trend of not moving forward in your walk with Jesus. If frustration doesn't set in, then a numbing slumber starts to blanket your life.

In order to break through this lifestyle of mediocrity, you have to wake up to the honest truth of where you are and where you are not. An accountant would call this awakening a precise audit. A teacher or your doctor would call this a complete assessment, and only after the test results are in can you know if and where a change is necessary in order to move forward.

In a similar fashion, many churches find themselves in a time of massive change. Modern society in the United States, in general, is no longer encouraging or even embracing Christianity. Nationwide, traditional church memberships have largely been declining. Morality is on a downward slide, even in the Church, and new laws are antagonistic toward believers. Churches and their members are overloaded with financial debt and too bankrupt on time to focus on the important areas of life. Many feel so beaten down that even if they went to church, they want only to be encouraged and made to feel happy, rather than to be confronted with the truth of their sin. Entertainment and media have set such a high standard that some churches feel they can't compete in drawing or keeping the attention of people hungry for a quick-fix of fun and entertainment.

Remember the strong words Yeshua spoke to the seven churches in the early chapters of the book of Revelation? I wonder what He would say about the state of the Church in America and much of the world today. *Selah.*

And yet, surely there would be quite a few things that would bring a smile to His face. No doubt! More people are being exposed to Jesus than ever before in the history of the planet. Although the Internet is littered with some of the most abominable poison our culture has to offer, it also hosts great news about the King of Kings reaching the uttermost parts of the earth. God's Spirit is bringing conviction and enlightenment. People are seeing healing and salvation from Messiah. The gifts of the Holy Spirit and the fruit of the Spirit are spreading like wildfire in many parts of the world! While some churches and believers are missing out, there are many moving forward in advancing the Kingdom of God all over the earth!

Consider some of these amazing testimonies of churches, ministries, and people serving Jesus Christ in the past twenty-five years:

- As of the first printing of this book, Reinhard Bonnke's ministry, Christ for all Nations, has seen more than 75,000,000 decision cards from people accepting Jesus Christ as their Lord and Savior! This has been happening heavily in Africa, but it is also occurring throughout the world. And these new believers are being funneled into local churches.
- Christian music has experienced explosive growth as an industry worldwide! But even more important, it has blessed, provoked, and enabled Christians to grow in their intimacy with their Savior. People are worshipping from their heart by the hundreds of millions! In Wilbur Ministries, we are seeing God powerfully move as never before on the six continents in which we minister each year! Millions of our CDs and DVDs are used and experienced in places like Thailand, Russia, and Mainland China!
- Campus Crusade for Christ in the United States has impacted the world through its movie *The Jesus Film*.

This is the world's most translated film, now shown in 1,300 languages in every nation in the world! To date, it is responsible for 6.5 billion exposures of the gospel and 230 million have indicated decisions for Christ.

- The publishing and production of Christian books, eBooks, YouTube channels, and films are going through the roof as new resources and methods of sharing the gospel multiply with every new medium.
- Millions of websites, blogs, and Facebook pages are engaging people worldwide on computers and mobile devices, presenting the hope found in our Messiah!
- And the list goes on and on…

But what would God's concerns be today as He looks at the Body of Messiah here in the West?

I believe God would be baffled by how anyone can read His Word and live a gospel other than the one He clearly put forth. Today our nation is filled with an easy-believism gospel, which offers the full range of the benefits of salvation, without a need to change our lives through true repentance or submission to the leadership of the Holy Spirit. Some have reached out during a time of need—receiving Yeshua as Savior, but not going all the way to make Him Lord of their lives.

A critical component of the Good News is the absolute need for repentance. True repentance includes:

- A clear recognition that our sinful actions violate God's just and revealed standards
- The need to confess our specific sins
- A deep, heart-felt godly sorrow for sinning against God
- A decision and resolve to turn away from these actions/ thoughts that separate us from God
- Determined action to live differently, in accordance to God's leadership

- Commitment to gain God's perspective on offending issues, making it our new perspective

I believe all the above can be boiled down to this simple statement: *Love what God loves and hate what He hates.* But some would argue, how can a mere man have the same mind or opinion as God almighty? In 1 Corinthians 2:16, the apostle Paul takes this argument on toe-to-toe, as he quotes Isaiah, the prophet, in chapter 40, who asks the very same question. Paul then finishes the argument with a very simple statement: *"But we have the mind of Messiah."*

Too many people are basically told to just repeat these magic words: "Jesus, I goofed up. Sorry. Forgive me. Save me. Thanks." From that point on, the person saying the magic words is given assurance of salvation in the afterlife. They are promised God's protection, huge successes, and over-abundant provision in this life. They are then invited to an amazing gathering (either in person or via TV/Internet), filled with incredible lighting, sound, and lessons on how to live more successfully. Groups are formed for any need or interest they may have, so they can enjoy and "better" their lives. And while those attributes are not wrong in and of themselves, do they actually hit the central mark of the gospel of Jesus Christ?

I am not trying to make light of a prayer for *true* salvation, but I am saying, let's be true to the *full* gospel when we lead someone to salvation through our amazing Savior. God sent His one and only Son into the world to pay the penalty for our violation of God's Law. Jesus poured out His life-blood, so each and every sin could be atoned for, according to God's rightful judgment. This is nothing to be taken lightly by people needing Jesus' supreme act of love. Jesus clearly lays out the plan for salvation, calling for the entry point of repentance from personal sin.

So what does all this mean for believers today? It means that true salvation will result in a radical shift. This means the Church of the living God should be filled with people who live according to biblical standards, not politically correct standards or self-oriented desires. No, this is not a gospel initiated and sustained by what you or I do. Rather, it is a gospel initiated by receiving the grace of God, and we continue to walk it out by the grace of God, in accordance to what the Bible shows as the "fruit of repentance."

Many churches preach a gospel of salvation that serves more as a check mark on someone's to-do list, rather than a stamp on a passport, which notes entry into a new country! Salvation is the stamp that indicates you have just entered into a new Kingdom, which operates according to the laws of that country! The laws not only define the things you must or must not do, but also the things you *get* to do as a result of being in that new kingdom!

But let's be clear, in many ways the church in America is operating according to some hyper-grace theology, whereby individuals get saved by grace and yet continue in their old lifestyle. Somehow God's costly grace, sending His Son to die for them, has now become their get-out-of-jail-free card, so they live any way they want. Dietrich Bonhoeffer, a German Lutheran pastor and martyr for his vocal opposition to Hitler's killing of millions of Jews, wrote in his book *The Cost of Discipleship:*

> Such grace is costly because it calls us to follow, and it is grace because it calls us to follow Jesus Christ. It is costly because it costs a man his life, and it is grace because it gives a man the only true life. It is costly because it condemns sin, and grace because it justifies the sinner.

In the hyper-grace doctrine, sin overshadows some new believers' responsibility to live according to the laws of God and His Kingdom. I guess they think Jesus' blood is sufficient to save them for eternity, but not strong enough to help them live a victorious and biblically-responsible life here on Earth. It's the ages old Savior and Lord argument.

When the apostle Paul wrote about believers walking in resurrection power, he meant it! The grace of God is displayed in His strength to overpower sin! Sometimes people mix up the words *grace* and *mercy*. Let's stop being a people who *always* require His great mercy. Instead, let's start walking in the power of His great grace! I really like the definition of grace I heard from John Bevere a few years back. He stated that we had completely misunderstood grace as we had been defining it for many years. Perhaps, like me, you have heard the simplistic definitions of grace and mercy. Grace was defined as receiving something that you did *not* deserve or earn, and mercy was *not* receiving what you *did* deserve or earn (because of sin). Bevere told us that we had always seen God's grace as His power to *forgive* sin, when actually the Bible teaches us that grace is His power working in us to *overcome* sin! I do like that! More grace, Lord!

Consider the amazing hope and expectancy for the Church today, which Paul describes in Romans 6:1-14 (TLV):

What shall we say then? Are we to continue in sin so that grace may abound? May it never be! How can we who died to sin still live in it? Or do you not know that all of us who were immersed into Messiah Yeshua were immersed into His death? Therefore we were buried together with Him through immersion into death—in order that just as Messiah was raised from the dead by the glory of the Father, so we too might walk in newness of life.

For if we have become joined together in the likeness of His death, certainly we also will be joined together in His resurrection—knowing our old man was crucified with Him so that the sinful body might be done away with, so we no longer serve sin. For he who has died is set free from sin.

Now if we have died with Messiah, we believe that we shall also live with Him. We know that Messiah, having been raised from the dead, no longer dies; death no longer is master over Him. For the death He died, He died to sin once for all; but the life He lives, He lives to God. So also continually count yourselves both dead to sin and alive to

God in Messiah Yeshua.

Therefore do not let sin rule in your mortal body so that you obey its desires. And do not keep yielding your body parts to sin as tools of wickedness; but yield yourselves to God as those alive from the dead, and your body parts as tools of righteousness to God. For sin shall not be master over you, for you are not under law but under grace.

The grace of God is the power of God to crush the sinful nature of man that opposes God! Jesus did not die for a powerless Church, but for one that would be the light to a dark and desperate world—a world hoping for real answers to real problems.

> Jesus did not die for a powerless Church, but for one that would be the light to a dark and desperate world.

During these difficult times, we are seeing the Church more focused on being blessed and learning life skills, than being focused on the matters closest to God's heart, as revealed in His Word. I'm sure each of you could give me a great list as to why this is occurring, and it would probably be right. But I'm going to take a stab at putting most of the blame into four interesting categories.

First, I see churches focused on *spectator Christianity*, instead of *participatory Christianity*. In my travels, I observe churches with professional staffs presenting believers with amazing worship services, cool lighting and sound, great counseling, and so much more. And that is fantastic! But the tendency for most believers is to think they themselves are either incapable, not educated enough, not needed, or even unwelcome to participate in the expansion of His Kingdom. Certainly, I am not blasting pastors in general, but I am pointing out a process that, if not carefully handled, will produce believers who just warm the chairs on Sunday morning (if convenient) and give their tithes (maybe). "Leave the heavy lifting of sharing the gospel, helping marriages, and dealing with the sick to the pros," the average member says. Although we all read the same Bible, somehow when it comes time to put our shoulder to the plow of the ministry, we think that surely those who are trained should be the ones to handle it. In other words, our expression of Christianity seems to take on more of a spectator-and-event tendency, rather than a personal commitment of involvement and action tendency.

The second characteristic that produces a powerless church is similar to the first, yet different. Somewhere along the line, we built a church of clergy, separated from what is called the laity. In other words, you are either a pastor type or you fall in the massive 99 percent of common believers, with no power, gifting, anointing, or calling to do the *real* spiritual stuff. Now, forget the fact that we are all common humans, saved by grace, and all have access to being filled with the same Holy Spirit. (By the way, this is the exact same Holy Spirit who was at creation and filled the apostles Paul and Peter...and for that matter, Jesus himself!)

When I read my Bible, I see a great commission to *all* believers in Mark 16:15-18, which authorizes and commands all (in the body of Christ) to do the work of the ministry. I read in 2 Corinthians 5:20 that we are *all* to walk in the authority as ambassadors for Christ. I could go on and on, listing every Scripture detailing who we are as believers, but let's just agree that God calls ministers to lead in equipping the saints *to do the work* of the ministry!

> *So Christ himself gave the apostles, the prophets, the evangelists, the pastors and teachers, to equip his people for works of service, so that the body of Christ may be built up until we all reach unity in the faith and in the knowledge of the Son of God and become mature, attaining to the whole measure of the fullness of Christ.* (Ephesians 4:11-13)

The third trait crippling our churches today is a non-sacrificial type of Christianity. "If church and ministry fits into my schedule, finances, and lifestyle, then I will try to get around to it." Perhaps we should just put the truth right out there—nothing great in life happens without a commitment to live sacrificially! Living successfully in God's Kingdom, as His son or daughter, will cost time, money, convenience, friendships, potential careers, promotions, and perhaps more. Yes, the cost, at times, can seem great…but the benefits are out-of-this-world amazing!

Everything in life has a cost. Of course you have heard the phrase, "nothing in life is free." In fact, both success and failures have a cost! Once you get over the concept that you are always going to pay, then you can focus on the issues that are really life-changing and important. Bottom line, do you really think God is going to ask you to sacrifice something (in any area of your life) for which He will not produce a Kingdom reward? Decide to live sacrificially for Him, and you will enjoy His goodness as He advances His Kingdom purposes.

The fourth and final characteristic harming us is that we try to make Christ *part* of our life, rather than *all* of our life. We tend to invite Jesus to help us in certain areas and solve our problems, yet we don't realize that we were bought with a price, and our life is not our own (1 Corinthians 6:20). When you were saved from the penalty for your sins, through the sacrifice of Jesus on your behalf, He did not die so that you would merely have life after death with the Father or even to have Him be your magic genie when you got into a jam. No! You were literally transferred *out* of Satan's kingdom of death and transferred *into* a brand new place called the Kingdom of God, which operates on God's Kingdom rules. You are now a citizen in His Kingdom, complete with all the responsibilities and opportunities. Not just a part of you, but *all* of you is to be involved in His agenda. Somehow the enemy of life has lied to modern believers and sold them a bill of goods that God is only interested in the *spiritual* part of their life. And, of course, Satan narrowly defines that as attending services and trying to be a good person. Wow, what a powerful deception that is, and it carries with it heavy consequences!

In my album *Your Great Name*, I sing a song entitled "Nobody Like You." The song starts out with the verse:

Lord of all, I bow down at Your feet
All to You, Lord I give all of me.

Our Lord does not desire a people, or a church, where the focus of life is not the King of Kings. Our Lord honors the humility of His people when they walk in a full-hearted trust of His leadership, seeking, and following His agenda. To yield all aspects of your life, your hopes, and desires, will not only invite the incredible presence of the Lord, resulting in your peace, but it will also bring His blessing, which is far beyond your imagination.

Radical shift from the fringe to mainstream, and the other way around

In our nation, and many nations of the world, the fringe of society has slowly become accepted, endorsed, legalized, and soon will be the mainstream standard of our brave new world. Seventy-five years ago we were a nation that shamed immorality, embraced Judeo-Christianity, and would not think about using tax dollars to support ungodly values.

Today, that has all changed. What used to be a small percentage of lifestyle choices within our nation, has now become the politically correct and governmentally endorsed lifestyles, or the law of the land.

> To yield all aspects of your life, your hopes, and desires, will not only invite the incredible presence of the Lord, resulting in your peace, but it will also bring His blessing, which is far beyond your imagination.

Sex outside of marriage is expected in our society. Talk show hosts and variety shows discuss not *if* but *when* sexual intimacy is proper in a new relationship. Protection, as opposed to abstention, is taught in our public schools, and even terminology that has stood the test of thousands of years and tradition, like "marriage," is legally changed and altered by our highest courts worldwide. We seem almost eager to embrace the most bizarre behavior among us, while rejecting the simple wisdom of God. Homosexuality is now promoted and protected as a politically correct lifestyle, along with gender change and the choice of public washrooms based on how you are feeling that day. "Educators" (I call them indoctrinators) are teaching our children in elementary schools to use their own judgment as to being attracted to members of the same sex, or consideration of changing their gender, or just playing out their fantasies. Pornography no longer has fringe acceptance but total mainstream emersion—in television, movies, literature, Internet, and gaming. Via smartphones and computers, pornography is viewed by a reported 70 percent of our nation (including adolescents) on a regular basis.

Christianity used to be the strong mainstream religion in America. But a 2014 Pew Research Center study, noting shifts in religion between 2007 and 2014, reported a strong trend decrease in the Christian share of the population within the United States. Non-Christian faiths increased 20 percent and Christian faith decreased by 10 percent. Most of the Christian decrease came from mainline Protestants and Catholics. Also, there was a huge 29 percent increase in a category named "Unaffiliated." The Unaffiliated category was made up of Atheists, Agnostics, and "Nothing-in-Particular."

The American value of showing deference to the minor percentage religions has now resulted in the fringe religions demanding equal, or even superior, footing to Christianity—in a nation founded primarily on the Judeo-Christian faith (although by professed numbers, Christianity slipped from 78.4 percent of the population to 70.6 percent). Society pressures now have the minority religions demanding superiority! Huh? Europe is now rife with Muslim "no go" zones for police and "non-believers" (or infidels, as we are all called), as the minority is quickly becoming a majority. If the Lord should tarry a bit more in wrapping up the ages, our children will certainly have a very different world to face than we ever dreamed possible.

And finally, let's talk money…your money. Specifically, let's talk about the money your government takes from your paycheck through taxation to fund the very programs you find outrageous. Now your tax dollars fund the reformation of your children's minds to embrace the ungodly principles of homosexuality, transsexuality, abortion on demand, and the rewriting of textbooks to remove exposure to historical information involving our Christian culture and beliefs. Your tax dollars will pay for litigation against your Christian beliefs and Constitutional rights. Your money, taken from your paycheck, will enable the promotion of the secular humanists' agenda as the religion of our land. In this great exchange of the mainstream becoming the fringe belief, let's consider the other side of the equation. Now the old mainstream of seventy-five years ago is being labeled the new fringe by the *old fringe*. For example:

- Historically conservative values are now viewed as "right-wing extremism."
- Christians with a voice in government are shunned, mocked, and marginalized.
- Businesses that used to respect a Sabbath or a Sunday are now open seven days a week, with no day of rest or time off for employees.
- Supporting Israel and standing against her enemies is now highly questioned by many and likely becoming a thing of the past.
- The re-interpreted Constitution, concerning separation of church and state, has basically relegated expression of faith to be a private matter, banned from public discourse and the marketplace.

Called to be a subculture...or a counterculture?

Merriam-Webster's Collegiate Dictionary defines a *subculture* as "an ethnic, regional, economic, or social group exhibiting characteristic patterns of behavior sufficient to distinguish it from others within an embracing culture or society."

A subculture embraces most or all of the values and ways of doing things as the larger society and is merely an identifiable grouping of folks with slightly different traits, housed within the culture at large.

A subculture is identified with, and usually submits to, the ways and mores of the larger culture that embraces it and permits it space to exist. Notice in this definition that a subculture exists as a group "within an *embracing* culture." When is the last time you felt that "warm embrace" from our society at large for being a Christian or Jewish voice to our generation?

Webster also offers another definition for a subculture when he states it is "a culture (as of bacteria) derived from another culture." I would give preference to this second definition if you were describing a denomination, church, or Kingdom society that has lost its saltiness and light. I would submit to you very strongly that the Kingdom of God was never birthed by Adonai in order to merely slip into some comfortable jammies and snuggle up with every king and kingdom that comes along!

A counterculture, on the other hand, is a group of people who profess beliefs, practice methods, and possess values diametrically opposed to the masses that surround it. In today's terminology, you might say that a counterculture is anything but politically correct!

So just for fun, let's paint a hypothetical picture of a church operating as a subculture. This would be a church made up of people who accept a fairly broad range of practices within their ideology. You definitely would not label them *radical* in their worship, evangelism and outreaches, discipleship accountabilities, or in meeting each other's relational or practical needs. The attendees come to church most of the time when convenient, and they might give time or money if they have extra. The Bible is a source of inspiration and offers good "suggestions" on how a person "could" live, serving as a wonderful guideline in decision-making. Their convictions seem more like opinions; they change with the times and are influenced on the whole by the society around them. Sunday mornings are normally enjoyed and lived differently than other days of the week. The members' calendars and checkbooks show their prime focuses are family, recreation, work, and career. They primarily vote for people they like or have strict party affiliation with, rather than voting according to moral or biblical standards. When people are sick within this church, the first place they look for assistance is medicine or doctors. In many ways, they look and operate similarly to a civic organization. Well that doesn't sound so bad.

At least they believe in God, right?

By contrast, let's look at a church and its members who operate in a countercultural way. This church appears more radical when contrasted to the subculture church described above. Members share a very sharp and well-defined standard for approaching all their decisions. They are unified in their beliefs and use the Bible as their *absolute* anchor and standard for decision-making. Appearances indicate that they worship with abandonment to God. They sacrificially give of their time and money to help others (beyond their family members), reaching them for Christ. The members hold small group Bible studies in their homes and give themselves to daily Bible reading and prayer. In fact, these people are really sold out to what they say they believe! God's power is regularly observed by people being prayed for and healed within the church, people seeing God's intervention in their finances, and the church reaching its community beyond its four walls. Their beliefs in the Bible are exercised in every arena of life, not just for sixty minutes on Sunday morning. Its members are willing to forgo promotion, inclusion, or opportunity, if called on to violate their beliefs. Their integrity in honoring God does not flex according to certain situations. They are definitely *not* politically correct. They are quick to listen, slow to speak, and slow to become angry. They demonstrate the Kingdom of God because they are disciples and imitators of God. You can pick them out in any crowd.

So what will it be for you—*sub* or *counter*? Consider these few lines from Paul's letter to the Ephesians before you cast your deciding vote.

Therefore be imitators of God, as beloved children; and walk in love, just as Christ also loved you and gave Himself up for us, an offering and a sacrifice to God as a fragrant aroma. Let no one deceive you with empty words, for because of these things the wrath of God comes upon the sons of disobedience. Therefore do not be partakers with them; for you were formerly darkness, but now you are Light in the Lord; walk as children of Light.

"Awake, sleeper,
And arise from the dead,
And Christ will shine on you."

Therefore be careful how you walk, not as unwise men but as wise, making the most of your time, because the days are evil. So then do not be foolish, but understand what the will of the Lord is. (Ephesians 5:1-2, 6-8, 15-17 NASB)

It's time to take a sober evaluation. Does your life convict others to walk in righteousness, or does it condone and encourage them to walk toward darkness? Are you ready to stand for what you say your convictions are? Will you stand with God's beloved Israel, when it is not popular and may cost you? Will you crush your fears of embarrassment or the possibilities that some won't understand, agree, or like your godly choices? Will you stand for Jesus, the persecuted One, even when the cost seems too high or the cross too heavy?

Will the real church *please wake up*! Jesus has called you, equipped you, anointed you, and prepared you for such a time as this because…

a King is coming!

CHAPTER 7

Navigating in an Anti-Semitic and Anti-Christian World

Imagine for a moment that your city has been invaded by a foreign power. Suddenly, the revelation hits you like a brick between your eyes—you are now living behind enemy lines! All your senses are on high alert. You begin to think differently; you prepare for your days differently. Opposition is now expected; your very life hangs in the balance. And this has become your new norm.

Unfortunately, many in this world can relate to the above imagery because it is their daily reality. However, most of us in the United States have to stretch our imaginations to even consider this concept. Yet, as followers of Christ, we do live in a world occupied by a kingdom set directly against God almighty. That kingdom is hostile to the God of Abraham, Isaac, and Jacob. It is a massive coalition of unrelated people groups who have only this in common: They reject the God of the Bible and are captive to and influenced by the kingdom of darkness.

This coalition, which rejects the one true God and His agenda, is made up of Muslims, Hindus, and hundreds of other religions. Add to those, the growing number of atheists and agnostics who are immersed in their arrogant rationalizations. Then, mix into the coalition those who choose a sinful lifestyle over following the Bible's clearly revealed standards. After you blend all these together and further combine those who pledge allegiance to the god of self-centeredness, you have a world ripe for a leader to move against the purposes of God almighty.

The unseen leader of this massive coalition against the Kingdom of God is the very one who was booted out of heaven before recorded time. It should come as no surprise that Satan is behind this revolt in order to stamp out the Jewish people, the State of Israel, and the followers of Israel's Messiah. And as the signs of the times continue to point to Yeshua's soon return, the enemy is about to go "all-in" with every chip on the table. This is an all-or-nothing game for rulership of the universe; the real war for the Throne is being played out before our very eyes.

The clash of these two kingdoms, coupled with the realization that we are living behind enemy lines, should cause us to evaluate life from a very different perspective and adjust our lives accordingly. Naturally, given the environment just described, there would be a dramatic rise in anti-Semitism. We don't have to go back in history to recap all the horrible expressions of attempts to wipe out the Jews in Pharaoh's Egypt, Haman's Persia, Herod's reign and the Roman Empire, the Spanish Inquisition, the Russian pogroms, the Holocaust of Nazi Germany, or scores of other movements throughout the centuries. But it is important for us here to take a brief look at a few instances of anti-Semitism and anti-Christianity in recent years.

It should be noted here that in recent times when we mention anti-Semitism, we are also seeing anti-Christianity as a parallel force. Remember that Christians and Jews are the only two world faiths that worship the same God—Jehovah, the God of Abraham, Isaac, and Jacob. All the other religions of the world have their own holy books, shrines, gods, and holy days. Could it be that our common enemy is really doing us a favor by forcing us to stand together? Could it be that the common pressure from the world, along with the common cry for help from heaven, will reveal our need for one another and finally bring forth the *One New Man* Paul speaks about in Ephesians 2?

There have been worldwide drives to boycott Israel as a method of delegitimizing the country, crushing it economically, and turning the hearts of nations against the Jewish people. Anti-Semitism on college campuses has recently experienced resurgence in the name of Palestinian liberty and rights. Governments far and wide have "re-evaluated" their commitments with regard to Israel. Businesses have wrestled with the political correctness of affiliating with Jerusalem, in light of the clamor of the Palestinian movement. People on the political left and right have wavered in their support of Israel and are turning a blind eye to anti-Semitic gestures. The United Nations Security Council passed a resolution in December of 2016 to condemn Israeli settlement construction, while the United States chose not to veto this precedent-setting resolution.

The BDS movement—named for its call of Boycotts, Divestment, and Sanctions against Israel—began from a small Palestinian activist group in 2005. The idea was to pressure businesses and governments into boycotting interactions with Israel, divest of interests inside of Israel, and actually sanction the Jewish state. Multinational businesses felt the pressure, and many succumbed to dropping Israel as a partner. Some entertainers stopped going to Israel, and sadly, a couple of Christian denominations joined the movement, like the United Church of Christ and the Presbyterian Church (USA).

Sad.

"The real aim of BDS is to bring down the state of Israel," California State University professor As'ad AbuKhalil said in a 2015 *Washington Times* interview. "There should not be any equivocation on the subject. Justice and freedom for the Palestinians are incompatible with the existence of the state of Israel," he noted. (Question: Why do we allow haters like this to teach their vitriol on our college campuses, funded with our own tax dollars? Anybody? Cricket…cricket…)

Washington Times analyst Clifford May discussed the BDS propagandists' spin when he wrote,

Hamas fires missiles at Israeli villages and digs tunnels under Israeli farms to facilitate hostage-taking and mass murder; they call that "resistance." Israelis attempt to defend themselves; they call that "genocide." Close to 20 percent of Israel's citizens are Arab and Muslim. They enjoy freedom of worship and speech, cast votes, hold seats in the Knesset and sit on the Supreme Court. Nevertheless, BDS advocates slander Israel as "apartheid."

Anyone who is watching all this with a clear understanding knows that the proposed two-state solution to the Palestinian "problem" is the hoax of the century. Hamas, the Palestinian Authority, Hezb'allah, ISIS, and the nation of Iran all agree. When it comes to Israel, it is all or nothing. The common battle cry from these terrorists is always the same: "From the river (Jordan) to the sea, Palestine will soon be free!" These are not partners for peace. They are jackals, anxiously waiting for a carcass to pick clean, and their main partner in destruction, Iran, means to give it to them.

Lately, however, there are some today who are exhibiting some common sense, coupled with some laws with real teeth, crop up in the state legislatures here in America. Illinois and South Carolina saw passages of bills aimed at curbing this out-of-control BDS movement. In 2016, another twenty states are reviewing possible legislation. Four state governors in particular are championing the anti-BDS bills— Indiana's Mike Pence (now Vice President Pence), Florida's Governor Rick Scott, New York's Governor Andrew Cuomo, and Arizona's Governor Doug Ducey.

Governor Scott said, "The state of Florida will not waver in our support of Israel, one of our greatest allies and friends." At the signing of the bill, he emphatically declared, "The Boycott, Divestment and Sanction movement is fueled by anti-Semitism and has no place in Florida or any part of the world that values freedom and democracy." The Florida law prohibits the state from purchasing from companies that boycott Israel and its settlements and prohibits state investment in companies that support the BDS agenda.

"If you boycott against Israel, New York will boycott you," New York Governor Cuomo noted in June 2016, when he signed an order to direct state entities to divest all public funds supporting the Boycott, Divestment and Sanctions campaign against Israel.

Even former President Barack Obama, who typically would not be considered one of Israel's biggest supporters, signed an anti-BDS protection act for Israel in February 2016. Certainly the BDS battle is not over in this increasingly anti-Semitic world, by any means, but there are signs of hope on that front.

And, just today, January 8, 2017, in *The Washington Times,* I read that 109 Democrats joined 233 Republicans in the House of Representatives to change the disgraceful "abstention" of the Obama White House with regards to the U.N. Security Council vote in December of 2016. This is no small matter when there is such a large bi-partisan decision coming from our Congress members! It gives me great hope that our nation can be a sheep nation instead of following the goats off a cliff.

Meanwhile, on the campuses of our nation, it's another story. Pro-Palestinian groups continue to pop up and gain traction, even among students in the general university population who do not fully understand the scope or end-games of the movement. And many university administrators seem to be turning a blind eye toward anti-Semitic events, teachers, and dangerous situations.

In August 2016, *Accuracy in Academia* website reported an incident, which had occurred in May of 2016, that "involved an anti-Israel mob that disrupted a small event held by a Jewish student group on campus" at the University of California, Irvine. "The angry mob of about fifty students blocked the entrances and exits while loudly chanting angry, anti-Israel, anti-police, and pro-Palestinian sentiments that promoted violence, anti-Semitism, and hate. One Jewish student attempted to get away, but was chased and hounded by members of the angry mob, forcing her to hide in a kitchen while a UCI staff member protected her." After a three-month investigation by the UCI Office of

Student Conduct, the Students for Justice in Palestine organization was merely issued a "slap on the hand" in the way of a written warning. Typically, university officials go into high gear to solve reported hate crimes. Are these signs of the times in our higher educational institutions?

And then more anti-Semitism raised its ugly head at the 2016 Summer Olympics in Brazil. The delegation from Lebanon refused to ride on the same bus with the Israeli team. The Israeli team had to wait for the next bus! When Saudi Arabia and Syria faced opponents who represented Israel, both countries were willing to forfeit their chance to compete for Olympic medals. Most television viewers were shocked while watching the men's preliminary in Judo, as they witnessed Egyptian Islam El Shehaby refuse to shake the hand of his Israeli opponent, Or Sasson, following the end of the bout. Showing proper judgment, the International Olympic Committee ruled: "The Disciplinary Commission considered that [El Shehaby's] behavior at the end of the competition was contrary to the rules of fair play and against the spirit of friendship embodied in the Olympic Values." El Shehaby was sent home for his anti-Semitic actions.

And while anti-Semitism has been picking up steam in our world, so has a negative movement aimed at Christianity. Christians are heavily persecuted with increased brutality and at an increasingly growing rate, in Muslim and Hindu nations in particular. From Hindu India to the Middle Eastern or Indonesian Muslim nations, and from the "formerly" Christian European nations to China, Christians are being persecuted and killed at alarming rates. No longer are we dealing with merely seeing Christians *marginalized* in opportunities afforded, but we are seeing them crucified, shot, beheaded, crippled, and burned alive in cages and coffins.

There is an anti-Christian, anti-Semitic sentiment, which morphs into new politically correct laws aimed at castrating the beliefs and rights of Christians and Jews.

Consider a few of the headlines noted over the last several

months in christianheadlines.com:

- Three Christians Attacked by Hindu Extremist Mob in India
- China Churches Banned from Worship during Two-Day Global Economy Summit
- Christian Girl Burned Alive by ISIS Tells Her Mother to "Forgive Them" before Dying
- Growing Number of Americans Say Christians Complain Too Much about Persecution
- At Least Nine Killed in Philippines in Christmas Day Attack by Islamic Rebels
- ISIS Could Wipe out Christianity in Iraq by 2020
- Egyptian Christian Imprisoned for Handing out Bibles in Shopping Mall
- ISIS Extremists Execute Twelve Christians Who Refused to Renounce Faith
- Sudan Bans Freed South Sudanese Pastors from Leaving Country
- Chinese Government Continues to Crackdown on Churches
- Christian Mother of Three Kidnapped, Forced into "Islamic Marriage"
- Police Complicit in Attack on Christians in West Delhi India
- Syrian Christians Flee Swedish Asylum Amid Harassment from Muslims
- India: Christians Forced to Convert to Hinduism or Live in Poverty

No longer is this problem somewhere else out there in the world, but here at home in the United States there is an anti-Christian, anti-Semitic sentiment, which morphs into new politically correct laws aimed at castrating the beliefs and rights of Christians and Jews.

But this persecution should not take us by surprise. Jesus clearly warned us that these days would come, and we should prepare our hearts and lives for times like these. But His focus was not just that we would be able to endure these tumultuous times, but also that we would recognize these times as our *signal* to whole-heartedly *engage* in being a part of advancing His Kingdom on Earth as it is in heaven!

Recently I watched the 2016 Summer Olympics—specifically the relay races—as nation competed against nation. When the baton was passed to the last runner of each team in the relay, that individual realized that whatever had happened in the race prior to that moment of receiving the baton almost didn't matter anymore. What was critical was what happened in this final push, the last leg of the race! And now we find ourselves in these end times, immediately preceding Messiah's second coming. The time is *now* for us to press in, regardless of the anti-Semitic and anti-Christian adversities of our day! And consider this, who does the coach choose to anchor the final lap of a race? Is it the weakest runner or swimmer? Absolutely not! He always chooses his fastest and best for the final leg of any race. And since these are "the days of Elijah" I guess that means that He has chosen you to be one of those anchor players to finish strong and carry the team across the line in victory!

But we need to press into all God has for us in a different way than we have in the past. As my dear friend Sid Roth has said many times, "It's not Judaism and Christianity, two streams of God, but the convergence of Jew and Gentile into one stream called the *One New Man*."

For He Himself is our peace, who has made both one, and has broken down the middle wall of separation, having abolished in His flesh the enmity, that is, the law of commandments contained in ordinances, so as to create in Himself ONE NEW MAN *from the two, thus making peace, and that He might reconcile them both to God in one body*

through the cross, thereby putting to death the enmity.
(Ephesians 2:14-16 NKJV, emphasis mine)

The apostle Paul knew that once the dividing wall between Jew and Gentile was abolished and the two groups could walk in unity, there would be an amazing outpouring of Messiah's resurrection power! An over-the-top revival would hit the planet of incredible proportions. Once this wall comes tumbling down, the mystery of Israel and the Church will be fully seen.

> *Now, therefore, you are no longer strangers and foreigners, but fellow citizens with the saints and members of the household of God, having been built on the foundation of the apostles and prophets, Jesus Christ Himself being the chief cornerstone, in whom the whole building, being fitted together, grows into a holy temple in the Lord, in whom you also are being built together for a dwelling place of God in the Spirit.* (Ephesians 2:19-22 NKJV)

Certainly the enemy of life does not want this new "spiritual dwelling/temple" to be put in place, so the devil's strategy is aimed at stopping the Gentiles and Jews from becoming this *One New Man*.

Quoting from my friend Sid again, "As we move toward a *One New Man* congregation, the Church owes a debt of gratitude to the Messianic Jewish movement. God used this rag-tag army of young Jewish believers in the 1970s to restore the Jewish roots of our faith." Very true…and yet there were some lessons Sid pointed out that we learned from those early days of the Messianic Jewish movement. Sid went on to explain:

In our immaturity, we overreacted in our Jewishness. We thought Jewishness was similar to the traditional synagogue's style of worship. We were resisted and misunderstood by the Gentile church. Both traditional

Jews and Christians viewed us as a cult. We thought that the more Jewish we appeared, the more acceptable we would be to the Jewish community. But we didn't reach many traditional Jews. Unintentionally, as we tried to reach traditional Jews, we made Gentile believers who loved us feel like second-class citizens. We had good intentions, but our stance was unbiblical, and this I regret.

There is enough anti-Semitism in this world without Messianic believers facing it from the Gentile Church, too. And there is enough anti-Christianity facing the Gentile Christian Church without Messianic Jews not fully embracing their Gentile brothers in Yeshua. The key concept here, I believe, is "humility." Psalm 133:1 says, *"Behold how good and how pleasant it is for brothers to dwell together in unity."* The last verse of this well-known passage declares, *"for there the Lord will command His blessing, even life forevermore."* The message here is so clear to me; no humility, no unity, no unity…no blessing.

So this *One New Man* is facing a kingdom of darkness purposed to destroy and render us useless in reaching the lost, hurting, and broken. Jews and Christians alike must stand together against the world's anti-God forces, intent on ushering in all forms of evil. Whether these enemies are anti-Semitic or anti-Christian, their real goal is to deny the plans and purposes of Yeshua our Messiah.

In order for us to truly advance the Kingdom of God, we need to be certain we properly identify the true enemy of our souls, and at the same time, lock arms with our true brothers in Messiah. Scripture says in Ephesians 6:12: *"For our struggle is not against flesh and blood, but against the rulers, against the authorities, against the powers of this dark world and against the spiritual forces of evil in the heavenly realms."* I have heard it said that a godly man will "cover his brother and expose the enemy." Far too often, I believe, we have been guilty of exposing our brother (to judgment and ridicule), while covering the enemy in our midst who comes only to steal, kill, and destroy us!

Writing to the Gentile church in Rome, the apostle Paul said:

I do not want you to be ignorant of this mystery, brothers and sisters, so that you may not be conceited: Israel has experienced a hardening in part until the full number of the Gentiles has come in, and in this way all Israel will be saved. As it is written:

"The deliverer will come from Zion; he will turn godlessness away from Jacob. And this is my covenant with them when I take away their sins." (Romans 11:25-27)

The Jewish people will play a *huge* part in the soon-approaching end times. As the full number of Gentiles come into God's Kingdom, there will be a great awakening within the Jewish world as they recognize and accept their Messiah Yeshua. Nations who embrace and bless Israel will be blessed, and those that curse Israel will receive the wrath of God (see Genesis 12:1-3). As the *One New Man* congregation unites, the overwhelming power of God will flow, and a massive revival will happen as battle lines are drawn between the people of God and the followers of the anti-Christ.

> As the *One New Man* congregation unites, the overwhelming power of God will flow, and a massive revival will happen as battle lines are drawn between the people of God and the followers of the anti-Christ.

The times will not be easy during the seven years of tribulation. The circumstances will look dire. Many will be fearful and confused; many will turn away. Some will trade the truth they cannot see for the lie that they can see.

Why the confusion? Some don't truly know God, and the truth eludes them. Some who do know Him, don't really believe His Word. Some hearts will fail them for fear.

So what are some strategies to successfully navigate in this increasingly anti-Semitic, anti-Christian world? What are different ways you can insulate yourself against the coming onslaught of anti-God sentiment and pressure? There are probably dozens of answers, but I am going to reduce them down to three simple ones, which you can immediately implement with great success.

First, love the Lord your God with all your heart, soul, strength, and might. I could take several volumes to expound on this phrase, but suffice it to say, be an imitator of Messiah Yeshua.

Second, love what God loves and hate what He hates. We need to develop the "mind of Messiah" in all things. Through prayer, praise, and the intake of his Word, we can have the same mind that was in Yeshua Himself.

Third, live a life of love displayed toward all men everywhere. Be an active part of God's *One New Man* congregation (Ephesians 2:14-16). Seek out, embrace, and co-labor with other believers to advance His kingdom during these anti-God times. Buckle your seat belt and enjoy the ride!

Love God, love people, because...

a King is coming!

CHAPTER 8

Continuance, Not Replacement

A s I consider the Word of God as a whole, several thoughts come to mind. I wonder if in the great scheme of things, whether God didn't foresee something happening with regards to Israel and was forced to develop a Plan B, as in the case when many Israelites initially rejected Jesus as the Messiah. I'm curious about the tipping-point where God's grace is not sufficient to forgive and restore. Where is the red-line to God's patience with a people with whom He chose to be in covenant? And when Adonai uses terms like *forever* and *eternal*, does He really mean forever and eternal?

So where and how do the Jewish people fit into God's plan in relation to the Christian Church? Where you come down on this issue will have a profound impact on the Church's power, love, and outreach to unbelievers in these end times! Is the Church today a *continuation* of God's work that has come through the people of Israel, or has the Jew been dumped by God and replaced by the Gentile Church? Can God's covenant with Abraham and his seed (Genesis 15) coexist with the New Covenant, or has one been replaced by the other that is better, newer, shinier, and more relevant?

There is an erroneous theology that has sought to provide correct answers to a lot of these questions, but as you will clearly see, it fails to do so. This teaching is called *replacement theology*. It has actually been around for a long time and is still popular today in some circles. Simply stated, replacement theology is the belief that because of Israel's rejection of Jesus as their Messiah, God has forever rejected the Jewish people, has taken away Israel's covenant blessings, and has given those blessings to the Church. In other words, this teaching states that the Church has replaced Israel.

In replacement theology, it is thought that the Jews are no longer God's chosen people, and after Pentecost in Acts 2, all references to Israel are now understood as belonging to the Church, which is now called "spiritual Israel." According to this teaching, the Jews have now forfeited their calling, and all the covenants and blessings initially given to Israel have been stripped away and given to the Church. But is this *really* what the Scripture teaches? How did this gross doctrinal error come about in the first place? When did it start?

First, let's note that replacement theology did not come primarily from unbelievers like atheists, agnostics, or even from other religions. It came from the budding Christian community after the First Jewish Revolt in AD 66. Prior to that time, the Roman world considered Christianity as basically a sect of Judaism, as were the Pharisees, Sadducees, and Essenes. In fact, the earliest believers in Messiah were *all* Jewish and were called "Nazarenes," as they followed the Rabbi from Nazareth. I have heard some Rabbinic Jewish scholars admit that as many as one-sixth of Israel's population, or one million Jews, followed Yeshua as Messiah after the resurrection! In the first century, and until this Jewish revolt took place, the Church was well-connected to its Jewish roots. But after the revolt, a significant separation began. Jews didn't want to be identified as Christians, and Christians didn't want to be identified as Jews. You see this at the birth of the Christian Church in Acts, chapter 2, and the division only grew from the middle of the first century on.

After the Second Jewish Revolt (AD 132-135), which was ended by the Roman Emperor Hadrian, the theological and political power began to shift from Messianic Jewish leaders to the centers of Gentile-Christian leadership in Alexandria, Rome, and Antioch. Though persecution of Christ-followers (Messianic Jews in particular) continued, the Church grew rapidly throughout the Roman world, increasing its numbers of non-Jewish members. As a consequence, Greek and Roman thought began to change the orientation of biblical interpretation, which was starting to be filtered through a Greek mindset, rather than a Jewish or Hebraic understanding. This change in orientation in biblical interpretation then brought about an even further separation. In AD 306, Constantine became the first Christian Roman Emperor. Initially, he afforded the Jews the same religious rights as Christians. However, in AD 321, he made Christianity the official religion of the Empire, to the exclusion of all other religions. This signaled the end of the persecution of Christians, but the beginning of discrimination and persecution of the Jews, and separation of Jews and Christians became more pronounced. Also that year, Constantine decreed all business should cease on "the honored day of the sun," and by substituting Sunday for the Sabbath as the day for Christian worship, he further advanced the split.[1] (For a much more in-depth study of this subject, I suggest you read *Our Hands Are Stained with Blood* by Dr. Michael L. Brown.)

As further division arose, it became very difficult for Judeo-Christians to hold onto their heritage and for Gentile Christians who wanted to learn more about their "parent" faith's Hebraic roots to hold onto their heritage as well. Anti-Semitic teachings, such as replacement theology, had been birthed within the Church, resulting in continued persecution of the Jews into the Middle Ages. What most fail to see in all this history is the reality of the enemy at work behind the scenes for all these years, scheming to keep the Jewish and Christian people apart. To be sure, this pain-filled history of the separation of Jewish and Gentile followers of Messiah is both heartbreaking and eye-opening. This is especially grievous when we realize that Jesus prayed that we all would be one.

By the way, Israel's rejection of Yeshua as Messiah does not result in God's rejection of Israel as His chosen people. In fact, Isaiah's famous 53rd chapter prophesied Israel's rejection and misunderstanding of the Suffering Servant. So according to this very specific prophesy, had Israel jumped on the Messianic bandwagon as a whole, it would have been the sure sign that Yeshua was *not* the promised Messiah!

Israel's rejection of Yeshua as Messiah does not result in God's rejection of Israel as His chosen people.

The truth is, the Church does have a familial relationship to Israel, as Israel does to the Church. We all just need to realize it and embrace it. For in God's mind, we are all one; the New Covenant states this very clearly. It says that the relationship of those in the Church, Jew or Gentile, is one of being "heirs" together of Abraham's Covenant of Promise: *"There is neither Jew nor Greek, there is neither slave nor free man, there is neither male nor female; for you are all one in Christ Jesus. If you belong to Christ, then you are Abraham's seed, and heirs according to the promise"* (Galatians 3:28-29). The key is belonging to Christ! The Gentile believer's relationship to Israel, according to the New Covenant, is that of being "grafted into" the true olive tree. Speaking to Gentile believers in Rome, God said, *"If some of the branches* [natural branches, meaning Israel] *have been broken off, and you, though a wild olive shoot, have been grafted in among the others and now share in the nourishing sap from the olive root"* (Romans 11:17, clarification mine).

The New Covenant states clearly that Gentiles have been "brought near," as in this passage:

> *Therefore, remember that formerly you who are Gentiles by birth and called "uncircumcised" by those who call themselves "the circumcision" (which is done in the body by human hands)—remember that at that time you were separate from Christ, excluded from citizenship in Israel and foreigners to the covenants of the promise, without hope and without God in the world. But now in Christ Jesus*

*you who once were far away have been brought near by
the blood of Christ. For he himself is our peace, who has
made the two groups one and has destroyed the barrier, the
dividing wall of hostility.* (Ephesians 2:11-14)

The New Covenant does not teach that we are separate, but rather
that Gentile believers are all Abraham's offspring, by virtue of our faith
in Christ, as seen in this passage of Scripture: *"Therefore, the promise
comes by faith, so that it may be by grace and may be guaranteed to
all Abraham's offspring—not only to those who are of the law but also
to those who have the faith of Abraham. He is the father of us all"*
(Romans 4:16).

Gentile believers are "partakers," Paul writes in his letter to the
Church in Rome: *"They were pleased to do it, and indeed they owe it
to them. For if the Gentiles have shared in the Jews' spiritual blessings,
they owe it to the Jews to share with them their material blessings"*
(Romans 15:27).

If the Church had understood the Bible's clear teaching from
the above passages, then the anti-Semitism from within the body of
believers would have never erupted. This teaching on replacement
theology would have never been a serious factor, causing the division
it did. In fact, it would do us all good to know the definitions of terms
when we speak about Israel, the Church, and the nations. Replacement
theology says that the Church is really the same "olive tree" as was
Israel before Israel forfeited her place with God. The erroneous claim
is that the Jewish people must be grafted into the Church, not their
own olive tree, according to the replacement theory interpretation of
Romans 11:17-24.

*But if some of the branches were broken off, and you, being
a wild olive, were grafted in among them and became
partaker with them of the rich root of the olive tree, do not
be arrogant toward the branches; but if you are arrogant,
remember that it is not you who supports the root, but*

95

the root supports you. You will say then, "Branches were broken off so that I might be grafted in." Quite right, they were broken off for their unbelief, but you stand by your faith. Do not be conceited, but fear; for if God did not spare the natural branches, He will not spare you, either. Behold then the kindness and severity of God; to those who fell, severity, but to you, God's kindness, if you continue in His kindness; otherwise you also will be cut off. And they also, if they do not continue in their unbelief, will be grafted in, for God is able to graft them in again. For if you were cut off from what is by nature a wild olive tree, and were grafted contrary to nature into a cultivated olive tree, how much more will these who are the natural branches be grafted into their own olive tree?

This Scripture clearly shows that Gentile believers are the "wild olive branches" who get new life from being grafted into the olive tree. The olive tree represents the covenants and promises made to Israel (Ephesians 2:12), rooted in Messiah Yeshua and nourished by the Holy Spirit, thereby giving life to the Jewish believers (the natural branches) and the Gentile believers (wild olive branches). Out of the heart of discipline, God "pruned off" many natural branches because of their unbelief and then grafted into the tree both believing Jews and Gentiles—*there was no replacement*. This truth maintains God's continual faithfulness to both believing Jews and Gentiles. Gentile believers are admonished to not be arrogant or boast against the "natural branches," because Jewish believers can be grafted in again. The olive tree root is not the Church; it is Christ. We are all grafted into God's plan of redemption—*One New Man* in Messiah.

Pride is a very tricky thing to deal with in a vacuum. It is hard to see when you are being deceived by its types and shadows ploy. We are all tempted to hope that our own tribe is the biggest and best. We place a lot of trust in the hope that we really are choosing the straight and narrow path, and we will defend that hope even unto death, if necessary. Yes, there exists something called Jewish pride, but there also exists an equally dangerous trait from the Gentile Church side as well. Nothing makes this point any stronger than the blind arrogance of replacement theology. Pride stinks no matter where you find it, because it emanates from the flesh of man and only produces more pride and more death. Of course the enemy of our souls loves anything that will cause division among us, and he especially loves it when it is fostered through blind pride and arrogance. Moses, John the Baptist, and Yeshua Himself were all upheld in Scripture as being the most humble among us. But consider this—it may have been Moses' one weak moment of pride when he struck the rock that caused him to be disqualified from walking into the Land of Promise. Pride is a killer; avoid it at all costs.

There is a great need to understand the destructiveness of replacement theology. The Kingdom of God is one of love and power, displayed by both Jewish and Gentile believers, walking in unity and humility. Some in the Church today have difficulty with Messianic Judaism because they believe it promotes two classes of Christianity. But it does not. In fact, the only difference between Israel and the Church is a matter of calling and identity, not a hierarchy of anointing or importance. Although both "natural branches" and "wild branches" are grafted into God's *One New Man* tree, there is a difference between the two branches, and that's okay with God. Believe it or not, God's heart is big enough to embrace and love both branches, regardless of the identity and calling of each.

The Kingdom of God has always worked best when Jews and Gentiles have put their hands together on the plow.

Consider this very important point as well: The Kingdom of God has always worked best when Jews and Gentiles have put their hands together on the plow. King Hiram of Lebanon was a close friend of King David, and when it came time to build a house for the God of Israel, Hiram sent cedar trees, skilled craftsmen, and more to help build a house for the God of his friend. Artaxerxes, king of Persia, released Nehemiah, Ezra and many others, along with money and materials, to rebuild the walls of Jerusalem that had been burned to the ground. The Kingdom works best when we submit to one another out of love for God.

One more little tidbit about this before moving on—a few lines back I mentioned the olive tree and the two branches. Did you know that in the natural world if you graft a wild branch into a cultivated tree, it will continue to bear wild fruit? The Kingdom of God is the only place where you can graft a wild olive branch into a cultivated tree (against nature), and it will bear cultivated fruit, the fruit of the Holy Spirit!

To further understand, let's take a look at just two of the many covenants God made with Israel—the Abrahamic covenant and the New Covenant—and how they can both be in place. The blood covenant, which God made with Abraham, was not a covenant that promised eternal life; the New Covenant does that. Specifically, the covenant with Abraham was for him and his *natural* seed to possess the land of Canaan and a promise that Adonai would be their God. Even today, God honors His covenant with Israel that is found in that bloodline— the sign of it being the circumcision of the flesh. The re-establishment of the State of Israel and the unprecedented homecoming of the Jewish people from the nations of the earth should be the strongest confirmation of the truth that God is still honoring this covenant for any God-fearing man or woman! Please read the Scripture below very carefully. The Lord said,

> *"I will establish My covenant between Me and you and your descendants after you throughout their generations for an everlasting covenant, to be God to you and to your descendants after you. I will give to you and to your descendants after you, the land of your sojourning, all the land of Canaan, for an everlasting possession; and I will be their God."*

God said further to Abraham, "Now as for you, you shall keep My covenant, you and your descendants after you throughout their generations. This is My covenant, which you shall keep, between Me and you and your descendants after you: every male among you shall be circumcised." (Genesis 17:7-10)

God made this covenant exclusively with Israel, not the Church. It is an everlasting covenant, and it includes an everlasting possession of the land for Israel. It is in effect today, regardless of Israel's current choice (as a nation) to not receive Jesus as Messiah. This covenant, along with others, can be in full operation simultaneously with the New Covenant, which most Jews have not availed themselves of *yet*. The New Covenant surpasses the circumcision covenant in great magnitude, yet it does not cancel out the Abrahamic covenant! And since that is okay with God, I think it should be okay within God's Church today. The covenant of circumcision promises blessing *in this life for the Jew, and in the land of Israel*, but it does not promise eternal life found solely through relationship with the Messiah/Savior of the world—Jesus. These are two separate covenants or promises that hold two separate purposes of God. They can and *must* coexist, according to Scripture!

God fulfills His promises; He doesn't cancel them. Let's take a look at Jesus's words that show how God fulfills and doesn't cancel:

"Do not think that I have come to abolish the Law or the Prophets; I have not come to abolish them but to fulfill them. For truly I tell you, until heaven and earth disappear, not the smallest letter, not the least stroke of a pen, will by any means disappear from the Law until everything is accomplished." (Matthew 5:17-18)

Before you conclude that "all has been accomplished" and therefore "passed away," consider that the word Yeshua Himself used here for "fulfill" is the Greek word pléroó, which means "raised to its highest expression." Now if we go back to this verse again and re-read it, inserting this meaning for "fulfill," we will get a very different interpretation than seeing it as accomplished in the sense that it has passed away! Here's how it reads with the Greek meaning for "fulfill":

> *"Do not think that I have come to abolish the Law or the Prophets; I have not come to abolish them but to raise them to their highest expression. For truly I tell you, until heaven and earth disappear, not the smallest letter, not the least stroke of a pen, will by any means disappear from the Law until everything is accomplished."*

Even concerning the Law and Prophets, God didn't cancel them; but rather, He fulfilled them by raising them to their highest expression in Messiah Jesus! (If you would like to learn more about this, please read my book, *Touching the Heart of God: Embracing the Calendar of the Kingdom*.)

One of the most exciting letters the apostle Paul wrote is the book of Romans. For centuries, Christians have loved the story of grace, salvation, and victory spelled out in the first eight chapters. But many thought Paul got ahold of some bad pizza and went on some kind of rant about Israel when he wrote chapters 9-11, finally regaining his flow in chapters 12-16—but nothing could be further from the truth! Yes, Paul wonderfully built an undeniable case for Christ in chapters 1-8, but those foundational truths were provided so he could address a serious concern in chapters 9-11. That concern was that the new Roman Christians were beginning to reject the Jewish believers, rather than incorporating them into the life-changing message and gathering of Jesus Christ. The seeds of replacement theology were beginning to be birthed in the Roman Church, and Paul was determined to bring correction on this topic before it could spin off into a full-blown anti-Semitism.

Paul was warning the Romans not to lose sight of the fact that God brought forth His Messiah out of Israel and that faithful Jewish believers carried the gospel to them in a faraway nation. He told them in Romans 1:16 that this gospel *"is the power of God for the salvation of everyone who believes: first for the Jew, then for the Gentile."* In his letter, Paul was going to build a case that the Jewish people were perhaps the *highest* example of God's grace. Even though they had a history of rebellion against the laws of God, the Father loves them, has a plan going forward that includes them, and still desires their salvation through His Son. After all, didn't Yeshua himself say many times that He had come for the *"lost sheep of Israel"* (Matthew 15:24)?

Perhaps second only to the grace God displayed through His Son on the cross, is the grace God displays to His chosen people—Israel. Despite their continual spiritual rebellion, God's love persists in His patience and pursuit of the Jewish people. As Paul revealed the heart of the Father toward the Jews in Romans, chapters 9-11, so should we yield to His heart today by cooperating with His Word. After all, who among us is without sin and not in need of the cleansing power of the sacrifice of Jesus? Remember, *"God so loved the world that He gave His one and only Son, that whoever believes in Him shall not perish but have eternal life"* (John 3:16).

The Roman believers were beginning to build a two-class Christian society. They were on the verge of judging their Messianic Jewish brothers and sisters, and by that lifestyle, they would be inviting the judgment of God upon themselves! Paul wanted to guard these new believers from falling into a trap of the evil one, while at the same time giving them sound doctrine for believing and living.

Driving home his point of accepting the Jewish believers fully into the Gentile-dominated Roman Church, Paul said,

> *"I ask then: Did God reject His people? By no means! I am an Israelite myself, a descendant of Abraham, from the tribe of Benjamin. God did not reject His people, whom*

He foreknew…Again I ask: Did they stumble so as to fall beyond recovery? Not at all! Rather, because of their transgression, salvation has come to the Gentiles to make Israel envious." (Romans 11:1-2, 11)

As a Jew himself, Paul let the Roman Church know as emphatically as he could, that God had no intention of dismantling His covenant of love for Israel. But God did use His expanded family of new Gentile believers to provoke the Jewish non-believers to jealousy as they watched this group of Holy Spirit empowered people worshiping the God of Israel.

Paul writes in Romans 11:28-29:

As far as the gospel is concerned, they [Israel] *are enemies for your sake; but as far as election is concerned, they are loved on account of the patriarchs, for God's gifts and his call are irrevocable.* (Clarification mine)

Did you catch that—irrevocable? In the Greek, the English word for irrevocable means *irrevocable*! The intent and call that God placed on Israel is still in effect. Jeremiah 31:35-37 echoes this by adding that God's covenants will stay intact, as surely as the sun, moon, and stars shine!

Dr. David R. Reagan, founder and director of Lamb & Lion Ministries, shared a great perspective on the Jewish people during these end times when he wrote on his website:

Keep in mind, the Jewish people are God's Chosen People (Deuteronomy 7:6). That does not mean they are saved. Rather, it means they were called by God to be witnesses to Him (Isaiah 43:10-12). Accordingly, when you study their history, you can come to an understanding of what it means to have a relationship with God. Their history shows that when you are faithful, God blesses. When you rebel,

He disciplines. And when you repent, He forgives and forgets and starts blessing again (read the Book of Judges). Currently, the Jewish people are under discipline. They have been for two thousand years. But one day soon their eyes will be opened to the reality of Jesus as their Messiah. When that happens, they will be overcome with grief, they will be swept by repentance, and a great remnant will be saved by grace through faith.[2]

And this brings us to three amazing things that happened as a result of Israel not initially receiving their Messiah:

- Israel became a light to guide the nations to salvation. (Acts 13:46-47; Isaiah 49:6)
- Through Yeshua, God made salvation available to non-Jews! (Romans 11:11)
- The Holy Spirit has been poured out on the people of the nations who believe. (Acts 10:45)

God's design for the Church today is *One New Man*, all saved and empowered by grace through faith in Jesus Christ. He established the true olive tree with the root of His Son, grafting in the "natural branches" alongside the "wild olive branches." Someone would have to ignore hundreds of Scripture verses to conclude that God is finished with natural Israel or the Jewish people. God is continuing His faithfulness initially displayed in the Hebrew Scriptures, or Tenach (the Old Testament), and now fulfilled and moving forward in the New Testament. It is a story of *continuance*, not a theology of replacement.

There are seventy-seven references to Israel in the New Testament, and not one of them refers to the Church. (Try replacing any of them with the words "the Church," and see if the passage still makes sense.) Israel means *Israel*—not "spiritualized" Israel.

Replacement, by its very nature, indicates that the one doing the replacing has the *authority* and ability to replace and acts upon it. So

I would ask then, on whose authority has Israel been replaced by the Church? The God-ordained covenants with Israel are *still* intact today. The New Covenant available *to the Jew first and also to the nations*, is still available today as stated two thousand years ago. A unified Church, empowered by the Truth, invites the power and blessing of God!

Let Your Kingdom come and Your will be done on earth because…

a King is coming!

[1]   "The Error of Replacement Theology" by Clarence H. Wagner, Jr., FocusOnJerusalem.com
[2]   "The Error of Replacement Theology" by Dr. David R. Reagan, www.Christinprophecy.org

CHAPTER 9

His Great Name
Will Prevail

We live in an information-overloaded society where it is way too easy to get overwhelmed, feeling like you are being force-fed to drink from the fire hose of breaking news, special alerts, and must have news flashes. These come at you from your computer, your phone, and your watch, while you are at work, driving, or maybe even trying to relax at home. This *life-altering* information is forwarded from your Facebook page, Twitter, email accounts, friends, and advertisers scrambling for your dollars, as well as politicians and even ministries who are vying for your attention. I feel like I need a hug just talking about the information invasion!

One hundred years ago, news was basically spread weekly, via newspapers alone. Then came radio, and soon television followed…to those who could afford them. I am old enough to remember when the only television available was black and white, and the few broadcast channels signed off around ten o'clock every evening with the playing of the National Anthem! I also remember when my best buddy, Kenny Prol, got a *color* TV around 1961…oh man! But today, via the Internet and smart phone technology, we carry in our pocket a non-stop flood of information, which is from the so called "mainstream media," usually opinion-driven and biased, rather than objective reporting.

Our perspectives about life are shaped by the input we receive and the people we allow to speak into our lives. Remember, the apostle Paul taught us in the book of Romans, chapter 10, verse 17, that "*faith comes by hearing.*" So what or who we listen to will begin to shape our opinion and our life choices, and we will only act upon that which we truly believe. Now add to this the fact that the enemy of our soul has stepped up his warfare against us and is influencing those who pump out the information stream that reaches us. With that, we have the making of a perfect storm. Our filtered society carefully spoon-feeds us all sorts of strategically-biased information, according to its own political correctness, based on an anti-God rhetoric, with a healthy dose of Socialism, and condemnation for anyone who doesn't agree with them, just because they can.

As terrorism intensifies around the world, and the persecution of both Christians and Jews is reported almost daily, it could be easy for hope to fly out the window. It would be normal to give way to a sense of inevitability because of the age in which we live and simply check out or disengage, believing we really cannot be any agent for good or change. It is easy to become discouraged, isn't it? We might ask, "Where is our Messiah in all of this? How long will Jesus tarry before He returns to judge the nations and set up His throne in Jerusalem?" Just a thought—is it possible that all this anti-Semitism and anti-Christian terrorism is happening at the same time in order to drive Christians and Jews closer and closer together? After all, we are the only people on the planet who worship the same God, are we not? And so, if we are not careful about where and from whom we gather our information, we could find ourselves joining the majority of politically correct, rather than the biblically correct.

Let me side step for a minute right here and tell you a story about my own struggles with the urge to forget about the fight and just battle for my own little space and family. In 2008, when the battle lines were being drawn for a new president to be elected, I heard in prayer, "As Ohio goes, so goes the nation." I believed that was a rallying cry for us to change our travel schedule and focus lots of time and energy touring Ohio and encouraging Christians to vote for righteousness. I hoped that believers would pray, hear from heaven, and vote for the candidates that most closely expressed their godly beliefs. That's not what happened. Evangelicals stayed away from the polls by the millions, Ohio went big for Mr. Obama, and for the next four years, we had a Democratic White House with the full control of both chambers of Congress that basically did whatever they believed was right.

Fast forward four more years, and we were once again in the throes of another national election. One day during prayer the Lord spoke to me again and said, "As Florida goes, so goes the nation." Okay, Florida, my home state…all right Lord, I've got this one. I have authority here, this is my home turf, so let's change our travel schedule and traverse the state, begging all who will listen to vote for righteousness! And so we did. Up and down the east and west coast, over to Orlando a couple times, south Florida into Miami, where the decision is usually settled because of population. And after the count, Florida went again for President Obama, and more than thirty million evangelicals nationwide stayed home from the polls.

For the next four years as I traveled around the globe, I asked the nations to please pray for the United States of America. In some nations, we literally turned our physical bodies as well as our hearts toward America and spent some long moments in prayer for this country. We prayed that the Lord would not necessarily give us the leaders we *want*, but the ones we *need* to move us out of this place we have made for ourselves, our children, and our children's children! Once a nation on a hill that sent the gospel to the four corners of the world and stood unwavering beside the nation of Israel, we were becoming a mission field ourselves of moral and spiritual equivalence. Our enemies no longer feared us, and our friends didn't trust us.

So when the presidential election of 2016 was heating up, and it was clear as mud where the whole thing was headed, we continued to sing, pray, and speak about American Evangelicals and Jews choosing for righteousness and not by what is heard in the media. The last week before the November 8ᵗʰ election, we were preparing to head to Israel and co-host a tour for forty-seven pilgrims anxious to see the land of the Bible. I remember voting a week early, as did my wife and children. Then on Election Day, my wife and I boarded planes for New York City and then Tel-Aviv, and the election results would have to wait until we landed in Israel late the following day. I remember telling the Lord, "If believers don't show up and make their voice heard this time…please don't speak to me anymore about elections in this country!"

When it was all said and done, and the choice was made (against *all* media reporting and biased expectations), Mr. Trump was declared to be the winner and the next president of the United States of America. A much larger percentage of Evangelicals had found their way to the polls and made their voices heard. When we landed in Tel-Aviv and heard the news, I looked at my wife and smiled. "So how do you feel now?" she asked. "This is the fruit you have been sowing on behalf of our nation for eight years!" The discouragement that I had been feeling for eight years, along with the temptation to just "give up the ship," all faded in a moment of realizing, once again, that the prayers of the righteous are powerful and effective, and they do avail much, for we are promised: *"If my people who are called by my name will humble themselves and pray…I will heal their land"* (2 Chronicles 7:14).

I love America. We are a deeply divided nation that desperately needs to return to the Author and Finisher of our faith and to the faith of our founding. I am hopeful once again that America will be one of those "sheep" nations that works with the plans and purposes of God almighty until Yeshua appears in the clouds and rules over the earth… let Your Kingdom come!

Don't misunderstand me here. Am I saying that President Trump is the messianic hope for America? Certainly not. Jesus is the only hope for America and the nations. However, when a man makes statements like, "It's time to bring God back into the White House," and I see him praying with Christian and Jewish leaders whom I admire…and I see him in large influential, Black churches and appointing well-known

God-fearing men and women for important leadership roles...hope springs up like a river inside of me. Hope that we have been given another season to believe and work for real change in America, which will turn all our hearts to the God who loves and established this great nation so many years ago!

All successful believers in Messiah choose to discipline their minds. They measure events, but not merely according to the media and those around them. Instead, they filter the events by what they already *know* to be true from a biblical perspective and by whose they are and what they believe! The apostle Paul said it best in this passage: *"I know whom I have believed, and am convinced that he is able to guard what I have entrusted to him until that day"* (2 Timothy 1:12).

So what do you *know* to be true about you? Here are a few encouraging thoughts:

- ADONAI—*He is the One who goes before you. He will be with you. He will not fail you or abandon you. Do not fear or be discouraged.* (Deuteronomy 31:8 TLV)
- *No weapon that is formed against you will prosper; and every tongue that accuses you in judgment you will condemn. This is the heritage of the servants of the LORD, and their vindication is from Me,"* declares the *LORD.* (Isaiah 54:17 NASB)
- *Surely I am with you always, to the very end of the age.* (Matthew 28:20)

Years ago, a man asked me, "What would you do, or who would you be if you knew you could never fail?" My answer was very simply, "I would change the way the world worships!" It seemed like a silly response from someone who had seldom left the shores of home and had no international platform from which to speak. Even my pastor at the time agreed that my answer was ludicrous. "Who do you know in the nations? How would you fund such an adventure? Has anyone called you to go to the nations? What languages do you speak?" These were all good questions for which I had no real answers. Then one day in 1994, a call came from Don Moen and Michael Coleman of Integrity Music. "We are here at a conference listening to Pastor Jack Hayford speak about the Psalms of Ascent that Israel would use to go up three times a year to worship the Lord. We want to go to Jerusalem next year and record a live project incorporating these Scriptures, and we believe the Lord asked us to call you and see if you might be interested..." After a short pause, so I could be certain I was hearing what I *thought* I just heard, my answer was simply, "I was born to do this recording." Within a few short months, "Shalom Jerusalem" was recorded live in Israel, and the nations were calling. Millions of CDs and DVDs later, produced in five languages, and we are still traveling the world with His life-saving message!

In my album *Your Great Name,* produced for Integrity Music, the title song, written by my friend Michael Neale, declares the truth for this hour and all eternity:

> *Lost are saved, find their way,*
> *at the sound of Your great name.*
> *All condemned feel no shame,*
> *at the sound of Your great name.*
> *Every fear has no place,*
> *at the sound of Your great name.*
> *The enemy, he has to leave,*
> *at the sound of Your great name!*
>
> *Jesus, worthy is the Lamb that was slain for us,*
> *Son of God and Man,*
> *You are high and lifted up,*
> *And all the earth will praise Your great name!*

There is a name to rule them all; there is a name at which every knee bows—the name Yeshua HaMashiach, Jesus the Messiah! Cancer is a name, but there is a higher name to which cancer must yield. Even hell, death, and the grave have lost their victory and must give way to the One who has conquered them all—the King of the Jews, the Lion of the Tribe of Judah, Yeshua, Jesus is His name!

As we read Scripture, many times it appears as if history repeats itself. And so it will be again, as our world faces deception and tyranny all around, pressures mount, and evil rises. There can be the "appearance" of certain destruction and failure. Yet looks can be deceiving when measured against the plans of God! Remember the story of Hezekiah, king of Judah, recorded in 2 Kings 18-19? Hezekiah was only twenty-five years of age when he was made to be king over Judah.

Hezekiah trusted in the LORD, the God of Israel. There was no one like him among all the kings of Judah, either before him or after him. He held fast to the LORD and did not stop following him; he kept the commands the LORD had given Moses. And the LORD was with him; he was successful in whatever he undertook. He rebelled against the king of Assyria and did not serve him. (2 Kings 18:5-7)

Hezekiah stood for God in the midst of a world opposed to its Creator. He didn't stand in thoughts and words alone, but also through courageous, follow-through actions. Much like today, the society around Hezekiah pushed an anti-God agenda. The mighty king of Assyria sent his world-conquering commander, Sennacherib, to attack and take over Judah. Backed by an undefeated record of conquering nations, and fueled with pride and arrogance against God and Judah, Sennacherib spewed out threats and intentions against God's people. In 2 Kings 18:33, the Assyrian commander arrogantly asks: *"Has the god of any nation ever delivered his land from the hand of the king of Assyria?"* How would it be possible for Judah to survive against this seemingly inevitable outcome?

Have you ever felt that our nation is facing odds so overwhelming that maybe we are beyond hope? Have you faced personal problems or crises so great in your own life that defeat would seem to be the only possible scenario?

> *When King Hezekiah's officials came to Isaiah, Isaiah said to them, "Tell your master, 'This is what the LORD says: Do not be afraid of what you have heard—those words with which the underlings of the king of Assyria have blasphemed me.'"* (2 Kings 19:5-6)

Words from our adversaries seem to carry great power, affecting our thinking and resulting actions. They minister fear and doubt and have the potential to discredit the intent of God's powerful spoken word. King Hezekiah knew God was with him, yet in the moment of verbal attack, coupled with historic evidence to back up his enemy's claim, the whole nation of Israel cringed in fear.

And yet, our enemy's words are just…words, and Adonai is still Lord of all!

After relentless assault and insult, the God of Abraham, Isaac, and Jacob would deliver His judgment against the Assyrians, backing up the word of His prophet, recorded for us in 2 Kings 19:32-35.

> *"Therefore this is what the LORD says concerning the king of Assyria: 'He will not enter this city or shoot an arrow here. He will not come before it with shield or build a siege ramp against it. By the way that he came he will return; he will not enter this city, declares the LORD. I will defend this city and save it, for my sake and for the sake of David my servant.'"*
>
> *That night the angel of the LORD went out and put to death a hundred and eighty-five thousand in the Assyrian*

camp. When the people got up the next morning—there were all the dead bodies!

Soberly consider the magnitude of what just happened in the passage above. There comes a point in time when God says, *"Enough is enough!"* In silence and fear, the Assyrians broke camp and left. God had heard the cry for help from His people, and He delivered them with swift justice. You see, God has an overarching plan for history that will be accomplished for His glory. His great name will prevail... against any and all odds; and it reaches to us in the here and now.

So as we consider our current situation and the state of the world as we know it, we might ask, "What is going on, and is there any hope for deliverance coming anytime soon?" Know that the signs and signals are evidence that a King is coming. Know that what is happening in the Middle East, in the United States, and in all the nations of the world, are the labor contractions of another great birth...the Kingdom of God is at hand!

In the same album mentioned earlier in this chapter, I sing a song of victory entitled *Mighty and Glorious*. This song captures my heart every time I sing it around the world, and it reminds me where and with whom the victory lies. It summons a shout from my spirit-man because it reminds me that the battle belongs to the One who has never been defeated!

Mighty and glorious, You are victorious
O God the sovereign and strong.
Exalted and powerful, fearful and wonderful,
O God the Infinite One.
We cry holy, holy is the Lamb!

As this great shaking takes place all around us, we must be fully convinced and stand on the Rock of our Salvation, *knowing* that He is sovereign, He is the definition of strength, and He is always victorious! He alone is the great deliverer of His people who receive Messiah—both Jew and Gentile.

Dr. David R. Reagan, founder of director of Lamb & Lion Ministries, summarized God's plan for end-time Israel when he wrote on his website:

> It is only when you understand how much God loves the Jewish people and how determined He is to bring a great remnant to salvation, that you can begin to understand what is going on in the Middle East today. The Bible clearly reveals that the 20th Century re-gathering of the Jewish people from the four corners of the earth back to their homeland is a supernatural act of God that is the first step in bringing about the salvation of the remnant (Isaiah 11:10-12). Specifically, the Scriptures teach that once the Jews are re-gathered in unbelief and their nation is re-established, God will bring all the nations of the earth against them over the issue of who is going to control Jerusalem (Zechariah 12:2-3).

But before the great and terrible day of the coming of the Lord, there will be a severe clashing of light and darkness, even greater than what we are seeing today. In this confrontation, we tend to focus on the darkness of this world—this evil that so arrogantly appears throughout our society. If we're not careful, we could forget that when the light is shined into this darkness, it is the darkness—not the light—that *always* retreats! Darkness cannot hold its ground when God's truth shines into any situation. As it is in the natural, so it is in the spiritual. Scripture is loaded with illustrations where darkness encroaches on a person, a situation, or God's people in Israel, and the result is always the same... light chases the darkness.

In the great exodus from Egypt, do you remember the terrible darkness quickly closing in on Moses and the Israelites as they found themselves between a rock and a hard place? They were wedged in a death trap between Pharaoh's army and the Red Sea. Yet, was Jehovah fearful saying, "Oh no, what will I do now? I didn't see that coming?" Are you kidding me? He *merely* opened the Red Sea and said, "Let My people be delivered!" And then God crushed the entire army of Pharaoh, as the sea walls collapsed over the soldiers of the world's most powerful army when they tried to pursue the "helpless" people of God.

Remember in the book of Daniel, the young Hebrew captives Hananiah, Mishael, and Azariah, forced into service in Babylon, yet servants of the Most High God? King Nebuchadnezzar renamed them with the Babylonian names Shadrach, Meshach, and Abednego, and in fact elevated them in his service, due to their great wisdom and understanding. And yet, when darkness fell on Babylon's jealous leaders and they forced the king's hand into condemning the Hebrew slaves to certain death, Yeshua actually walked with them among the flames of the fiery furnace! The God of Israel delivered Hananiah, Mishael, and Azariah, crushed the evil intentions of the king, and showed the entire nation of Babylon that He alone can save!

Or what about the once proud and zealous Pharisee named Saul of Tarsus, who encountered the light of Yeshua while on his way to Damascus, Syria, where his intent was to arrest and persecute Jewish believers in Yeshua? When Jesus spoke to him that day, the presence and power of God was so strong that it literally knocked Saul to the ground and rendered him stone blind for days! He then became such a passionate follower of Yeshua that his letters to the believers in the first century make up two-thirds of the writings of the New Covenant!

Why all these examples? They are simply a reminder that the presence and power of God makes all the difference in any situation.

Personally, I have seen the movement of God prevail in the most difficult of circumstances. But one that makes my heart pound the most is when the Father touched my wife, Luanne. My wife had been afflicted for decades with a condition in her left leg called "lymphedema." We were told years ago by doctors specializing in this condition that it is pre-cancerous and spreads throughout the body, eventually taking over and causing painful swelling in all the limbs and face. Imagine how we felt. We finally found a doctor 1500 miles from our home who could help us. He told Luanne she would need to wrap her leg in layers of Ace bandage every day, sleep at night hooked up to a compression pump, and that there was no real cure for the disease. For more than twenty-five years this is how we lived, spending thousands of dollars each year on doctors, procedures, and equipment as we tried to deal with the affliction. Often the pain was so intense she would cry herself to sleep, and because of the pressure in an airplane cabin she couldn't accompany me on trips to minister. Of course we prayed and believed God, and many others joined us in prayer as well, but so often the answer seemed too far away.

And then one day as the Jubilee had come, I returned home from a ministry trip to see her standing in the doorway of our home, wearing *jeans* and the *same size shoe on both feet!* I cannot tell you the last time I had seen such a sight. I cried, she cried, and together we rejoiced in the King's faithfulness to take care of the kids in His Kingdom!

More and more as of late, people are approaching me after a service with reports of chronic pain leaving them, healings of all kinds, and many people are giving their lives to Yeshua. Healing, restoration, deliverance, whatever is needed for life and godliness is what my Bible says!

The light of God not only overcomes the darkness, but it separates the light from the darkness as well. It divides what is true from what is false, separates the soul and the spirit, and is even a discerner of the thoughts and intentions of the heart of man! Today a great separation is taking place. Those who are living in darkness are beginning to see a great light. It is not just from heaven, but also from the lives of those who have received the same light of Messiah Yeshua as those spoken of here:

> *"You are the light of the world. A town built on a hill cannot be hidden. Neither do people light a lamp and put it under a bowl. Instead they put it on its stand, and it gives light to everyone in the house. In the same way, let your light*

shine before others, that they may see your good deeds and glorify your Father in heaven." (Matthew 5:14-16)

Yes, His great name will prevail because His great power is carried in the lives of those who call him *Lord*. If you have a need…He has a name…call on the name of the Lord!

"For I know the plans that I have in mind for you," *declares Adonai, "plans for shalom and not calamity—to give you a future and a hope."* (Jeremiah 29:11 TLV)

He is in the process of finishing the good work He began in you, and He is using you to finish the good work of salvation He has begun in this world. Let your light shine bright because...

a King is coming!

CHAPTER 10

Worshiping in the
Waiting Room

What a journey we are on, preparing for a King of divine status who *is coming* to our planet! A friend of mine, Joel Richardson, wrote a book entitled *When a Jew Rules the World*, and it still shocks my intellect when I see those words. Yes, the King of the Jews is poised for a triumphal return. Many of the signs and events of our day indicate that this is imminent! The nation of Israel has re-appeared after millennia of the Jewish people being scattered all over the world (since AD 70)—Jews have risen from the ashes of the Nazi Holocaust, Jerusalem is back in Jewish hands after the Six-Day War in 1967, the Sanhedrin is re-established (which signals the rebuilding of the Jewish Temple and restoration of worship, as prophesied in the Bible), and the Church is coming alive. Make no mistake about it—God is definitely and pro-actively in the picture! This is *His* world and His time clock is announcing the second coming of His Son, not as a humble servant or sacrificial lamb to atone for our sins, but this time—as the conquering King!

...and in light of this, how then shall we live? (apostle Paul)

How can we worship the King while living in the middle of a battle zone? The Psalmist laments this same attitude in Psalm 137:4,

"How can we sing the songs of the Lord while in a foreign land?"
Without being too weird about all this, it's good to remember that this world is not our home. We do belong to another Kingdom and another King who is returning here to take us all home where we belong. But while we are here, we are encouraged to "make the most of every opportunity" and to be bold and strong, for the Lord is with us wherever we go.

There is a beautiful prayer in Jewish literature that I have recorded twice now. The first time was on the album *Your Great Name* for Integrity Music back in 2013. I recorded it just the way it was written by an ultra-Orthodox singer from Israel—in Hebrew. But the second time, I translated it into English so the rest of the world could enjoy the beauty and reverence of this solemn Jewish prayer. I paired it with the famous words from Psalm 118:26, *"Blessed is He who comes in the name of the Lord,"* and recorded it on the album entitled *Forever Good*. It goes like this…

Ani ma'amin, b'emunah shelemah
B'viat, haMashiach ani ma'amin
I believe with perfect faith in the coming of Messiah
And even though He may tarry, yet will I wait for Him every day.

In this book, I have sought to expose what has been going on in the seen (natural) and the unseen (spiritual) realms of this world. All the signs and events I have written about are a preamble to the King of Kings returning to receive His Bride and setting in place His everlasting rule over both heaven and earth. Political unrest, nation rising up against nation, abandonment of Israel by allies, morality crises, and arrogance against the Almighty have all been shown to be the prophetic outworking of the days in which we live. So as we find ourselves swimming in these soul-devouring, shark-infested waters, where can we find the safe houses of peace, perspective, and purpose? How are we to live in these dangerous waters, while waiting on the King's return?

Christ has made a way for us to be the victors and not the victims in these times. We must realize that we live in a different reality than what is seen in this world, and we are messengers of that different reality. What do I mean by that? Just like Abraham, we are sojourning by faith, "looking for a city." Paul said that our citizenship is in heaven, that we have been translated into the Kingdom of the Son. We are a part of that Kingdom now, and as believers, we are to operate from the power and principles of that Kingdom. We have authority given to us from the King. We have His name. We are victors holding forth the Word of Life in the midst of a crooked and perverse generation. So our message and our actions, the way we live and minister, are truly from a *different reality*—it's from *God's reality*! Let me share with you an experience to show how this is lived out.

Recently, I went with my family to one of our favorite lunch stops in Jacksonville, Florida. The owners are Jewish, and I have testified to them for years and asked them to join us for a Shabbat service when they could. One of the owners came to me and said he was leaving the country for medical treatments on his back that he couldn't get here in the States. He is not a religious man, he just went through a painful divorce, and now his body is breaking down in constant pain. "Enough already!" I stated rather loudly in his crowded deli. "Sit down here, because I want to pray for you!" I reminded him that it is almost Hanukkah, the time for miracles, and that he was one of the "chosen" and in line for a miracle that would change his life. So we all bowed our heads, and I prayed for his restoration—body, soul, and spirit. He was grateful for the prayer and concern. I bet no one had ever prayed for him in his entire life!

Friend, it doesn't matter what the people (or the governments) of this world think about Jesus and the cross. It doesn't matter whether they accept our God-reality or not, though we certainly want them to. Paul said, *"For the message of the cross is foolishness to those who are perishing, but to us who are being saved it is the power of God"* (1 Corinthians 1:18). As Believers, we are victors, and we have authority and power through the Holy Spirit in this life. We are the head and not the tail, above and not beneath, and we can exhibit the reality of Christ in us and through us because it is the truth. It is what God's Holy Word says about us, and we can live our lives accordingly. That day when I prayed for my friend, I was coming from a *different reality* because of *Jesus in me*. I am sure that my Jewish friend was blessed that day because I was operating from that reality.

So getting back to the matter of how we can effectively live and worship in the midst of crisis, here are four strategies to help us live as victors and not victims:

- Get into His presence daily, He is a strong tower of safety.
- Live what you believe
- Navigate through troubled waters using God's tools.
- Discipline your mind to focus on the important things of life.

Get into His presence daily, He is a strong tower of safety

More than twenty years ago, I recorded the album *Shalom Jerusalem*, and in it I sang a song that has brought comfort and peace to thousands of people around the world during times of trouble and sorrow. When I recorded Lynn DeShazo's song "In Your Presence O God," it was more than a song of worship and comfort; it also became an anthem for a victorious declaration of truth. These lyrics have become a sure and deep-rooted foundation not only for me, but to millions who have sung them and allowed the truth of them to soak deep into their souls. These words form the only environment I know from which to view life correctly. They are like putting on the correct prescription glasses in order to gain the most accurate perspective of what is happening around me. Read these words and allow them to wash over your heart and mind.

In Your presence, that's where I am strong;
In Your presence, O Lord my God.

In Your presence, That's where I belong;
Seeking Your face, Touching Your grace
In the cleft of the Rock...In Your presence O God.

I want to go where the rivers cannot overflow me,
Where my feet are on the Rock.
I want to hide where the blazing fire cannot burn me,
In your presence O God.

I want to hide where the flood of evil cannot reach me,
Where I'm covered by the blood.
I want to be where the schemes of darkness cannot touch me,
In Your presence O God.

You are my firm foundation, I trust in You all day long.
I am Your child and Your servant,
And You are my strength and my song.

In Your presence, that's where I am strong;
In Your presence, O Lord my God.
In Your presence, That's where I belong;
Seeking Your face, Touching Your grace
In the cleft of the Rock...In Your presence O God.

Those of you who have listened and meditated on this song before find yourselves singing it in your heart right now, I bet. I have found that it is only by pressing into His presence that a person can begin to gain godly perspective in the middle of a crisis. When emotions are high, as the tides of fear and uncertainty rise, our vision and understanding of circumstances can become skewed. It is normal and natural in these times to find ourselves either overwhelmed and stopped in our tracks, or making decisions birthed out of panic, or the feeling that we must take matters into our own hands.

Yet our God has another method for navigating life, despite the personal and national crisis all around. It is *experiencing His presence daily*. For us to hear from Him, we must quiet our souls and draw near to Him in worship and prayer. There is nothing that brings confidence of direction, or peace in the midst of troubling times, like *hearing* deep in your spirit from Father God. It is great to hear good advice from a mentor, a friend, or other person held in high regard, but nothing compares to the sense of well-being that comes from connecting to Jehovah-shalom, the God of peace. Imagine the confidence and peace you would experience, hearing these words during a time of crisis in your own life:

> *"I took you from the ends of the earth, from its farthest corners I called you. I said, 'You are my servant'; I have chosen you and have not rejected you. So do not fear, for I am with you; do not be dismayed, for I am your God. I will strengthen you and help you; I will uphold you with my righteous right hand."* (Isaiah 41:9-10)

So pull away from your daily grind and meet with God—get in His presence. Sacrifice what you must in order to silence life, just for a while, so you can have a heart-felt conversation with God and experience His interaction with you. Uncomfortable? Let me tell you, it is not as uncomfortable as trying to live life without His presence! Push yourself to draw aside. He is your Creator, He is your Abba Father. He is waiting for you.

Many years ago I was having one of those challenging seasons in life where I wondered who I was, what I was doing in my job, and when I would find grace for a life purpose. I was married and had a one-year-old son. I was working two jobs and still not making ends meet. I read many times in Zephaniah where God said He would sing over His people. Then one quiet morning, when I was by myself, I heard Him sing over me. I wrote down what I heard that day and have sung and recorded it many times since:

My soul finds rest in God alone, my peace depends on Him.
And in that place of quiet rest He fills me from within,
He pours on me His holy oil, the Spirit of Adonai,
Then He takes me by His hand and comforts me with His love
He comforts me with His love.

Those who wait upon the Lord, new strength He gives to them,
He gives them wings like the eagle, that they might soar with Him,
He weaves His strength into their lives, the Spirit of Adonai
Then He gives them all of His peace to guard their hearts and
their minds
Guarding our hearts and minds.

So come my soul now take your rest, come find your peace in Him
The holy presence of the Lord will fill you from within
O pour on me your holy oil, Spirit of the Living God
Fill my cup, Lord I lift it up, until I overflow.

Live what you believe

Yes, in unsettling times like these, we must discipline ourselves to regularly pull away for time in God's presence in order to gain an accurate perspective. But as it is with any relationship, the blessings don't come without responsibility. So I have outlined here five areas to be mindful of as we seek to love God with all our heart, mind, and strength.

First, don't dance with other partners! We are to have no idols—nothing or no one else we give our worship to; nothing or no one else we give our hearts to follow after. Proverbs 4:23 says, *"Above all else, guard your heart, for out of it flows the issues of life."* We think of "idols" in the West as a carving or an image that folks bow before. But as you know, it is all too easy to make an idol of a loved one, a job, or a degree, any number of things that get our best affection and attention. Our God is an awesome God, yes, but He is also a jealous God. He held nothing back when He paid the price for our salvation; therefore, He deserves no less than our total love and affection. Many believers try to make their walk with the Lord just a component of their lives. They compartmentalize, operating from different perspectives according to where and with whom they find themselves. The Bible calls this kind of person a *hypocrite*. It is impossible to please both God and your flesh. You can only serve one.

Walking with Yeshua in faithfulness will bring confidence and surety to your fellowship. What ease and satisfying joy there is when there is nothing hidden in a relationship! Let your affections and lifestyles reflect full commitment to your Lord, and watch Him protect and provide for you as He lavishes His love upon you. Clarity, direction, insights, and help, flow to the faithful, especially during times of trouble and uncertainty.

Remember Joseph, a young man with a heart for God? He saw visions, interpreted dreams, loved God—but that didn't guarantee him a standing ovation everywhere he went! Because he was painfully faithful, even when no one else was watching, the favor of God lifted him to the second highest throne of his day, where he saved the entire nation of Egypt and many others from starvation—including his own family who had persecuted him.

Second, Kingdom people need to be truly Kingdom people. No duplicity. Serving the King with integrity invites the provision and assistance of the King. In my last book, *Touching the Heart of God,* I described what it would be like to be a citizen in God's Kingdom. I described not only the responsibilities, but also the benefits of His Kingdom. And, oh, how the benefits are beyond compare! His Kingdom, made up of Jewish and Gentile believers in Yeshua, is intended to be *One New Man*, drawing all people to Him! When you were transferred from the kingdom of darkness to God's Kingdom of light, your new citizenship was empowered by His authority. His Kingdom purposes will prevail, not just in world events, but in your personal life as well!

But seek first his kingdom and his righteousness, and all these things will be given to you as well. (Matthew 6:33)

The third way to live faithfully is to follow Yeshua—for obedience is better than a sacrifice. As I travel the world, some people ask me what the secret is to living a successful life in the Lord. The simple answer is this: *Do what you are told.* It worked for Jesus, and I'm certain that it will work for us.

> *This is love for God: to obey his commands. And his commands are not burdensome, for everyone born of God overcomes the world. This is the victory that has overcome the world, even our faith.* (1 John 5:3-4)

Jesus's obedience is demonstrated by His own words:

> *So Jesus said, "When you have lifted up the Son of Man, then you will know that I am he and that I do nothing on my own but speak just what the Father has taught me. The one who sent me is with me; he has not left me alone, for I always do what pleases him."* (John 8:28-29)

Abraham's obedience to the Lord must have been agonizing as he raised the knife to kill his son Isaac on the altar that day. But then suddenly, God stopped Abraham and provided the sacrificial ram caught by its horns in the thicket. Then God spoke these words to him:

> *"Do not lay a hand on the boy," he said. "Do not do anything to him. Now I know that you fear God, because you have not withheld from me your son, your only son... and through your offspring all nations on earth will be blessed, because you have obeyed me."* (Genesis 22:12, 18)

A fourth part of loving God is "use what you have been given." One of my favorite *go-to* portions of Scripture for this is found in 1 John 2:20 and 27. When speaking to believers, the apostle John said,

"But you have an anointing from the Holy One, and all of you know the truth…As for you, the anointing you received from Him remains in you…" Each of us in the body of Messiah has been given an anointing, a gifting, a spiritual gift by God Himself, and He fully intends for us to use it!

Remember the parable of the talents? All three servants were given a sum of money to watch over for their master while he was away. Two of the men did well with what was entrusted to them, increasing their master's investment in them. But the third man hid his allotment out of fear. When the master returned, he took the treasure away from the man who did nothing with it and gave it to the man who had invested the five talents he had received. The master then called the third man foolish and wicked, and had him thrown outside into the darkness. The moral to this story is simple: Discover what you have been given, and use it for the glory of the Master.

The fifth area to be mindful of in loving God is found in 1 Peter 1:15, which says, *"But as He who has called you is holy, so be holy in all that you do."* By that, I mean that we have been called to be separate, set apart. Paul writes, *"Therefore if anyone is in Christ, he is a new creature; the old things passed away; behold, new things have come"* (2 Corinthians 5:17 NASB).

When I was a very new believer, I had more zeal than wisdom, and I couldn't wait to share my new life with my fraternity brothers back in Cleveland, Ohio. Finally, the opportunity came during a weekend visit with some friends, and a group of us went out on the town. It was so good to see the guys again. They could tell that something was different about me. We went out to an Irish pub for dinner and to enjoy some live music. The band was great, the food was terrific, and the company was wonderful. We reminisced about our years in college and all the dumb things we did. The problem was, one beer led to another…more chicken wings, more beer…and just as I stood to tell my friends sitting at the table why I had come…I fell backwards into the table behind me, and my testimony fell backwards with me! By the time I finally got off the floor and into the men's washroom, I was so ashamed. I cried out loud, feeling like I had embarrassed myself, and my King. The whole reason for my trip there was to share Jesus with my friends, who I truly loved and desired to see come into the Kingdom. I promised the Lord right then and there that if He would forgive me, this would never happen again. He did, and it hasn't. He also gave me another opportunity to share with my friends individually—with much better results!

Navigate through troubled waters using God's tools

Today, sea-going vessels use the latest in electronic navigation equipment to cross the oceans. But knock out a couple of satellites and ships would be in big trouble! For centuries past, sea captains used only two primary instruments to navigate successfully and stay away from danger—a ship's rudder and a sextant. The captain would steer the ship using the ship's rudder, while finding direction with the sextant. A *sextant* is a navigational tool incorporating a telescope and an angular scale, which is used to determine latitude and longitude. An astronomical object would be sighted through the telescope, and its angular distance above the horizon would be used to calculate the ship's position.

"Okay, thanks for the nautical lesson, but what does that have to do with helping me in a world gone mad?" you might ask.

To have direction in our world today, we, likewise, need two key tools: God's Word and the Holy Spirit. These two instruments will guide us to a safe harbor in a world that has lost its compass and destination. By the way, it is not either/or; we definitely need *both* the Word of God and the Holy Spirit in order to steer a clear course in life.

Wisdom, winning strategies for life, amazing mentors, and sound leadership can all be found in God's Word. Imagine custom-designed guidance—and it's all right there at your fingertips! Yes, the Scriptures are God's sextant to guide His people…they are also His *Owner's Manual* to fix, handle, and support any issue in your life.

Solomon, the wisest man who ever lived, orchestrated for us the book of Proverbs. It is loaded with wisdom to guide us in making good decisions in times of crisis. As an example of my encouragement for you to get into His Word, consider the first twelve verses of Proverbs, chapter 3. Just in these few verses you will find insights into:

- Living a long life
- Becoming prosperous and living in peace
- Finding favor with God
- Finding favor with those around you
- God making His way clear
- Developing a healthy body
- Strengthening your skeletal system
- Having more income and provision than you were prepared for
- Receiving insight, discipline, and correction from the Lord
- How to receive God's love

My son, do not forget my teaching, but keep my commands in your heart, for they will prolong your life many years and bring you peace and prosperity. Let love and faithfulness never leave you; bind them around your neck, write them on the tablet of your heart. Then you will win favor and a good name in the sight of God and man. Trust in the Lord with all your heart and lean not on your own understanding; in all your ways submit to him, and he will make your paths straight. Do not be wise in your own eyes; fear the Lord and shun evil. This will bring health to your body and nourishment to your bones. Honor the Lord with your wealth, with the first fruits of all your crops; then your barns will be filled to overflowing, and your vats will brim over with new wine. My son, do not despise the Lord's discipline, and do not resent his rebuke, because the Lord

disciplines those he loves, as a father the son he delights in.
(Proverbs 3:1-12)

The Word of God, sharper than any two-edged sword, divides between what is true and false, the soul and the spirit, and is a lamp for our feet, a light for a dark path...powerful! I remember when I was first born again and the Word came alive to me. I began to memorize a verse every week, then two or three, then a whole chapter. I found myself addicted to the fellowship of the Holy Spirit, and I grew by leaps and bounds. Answers to difficult questions seemed to flow from nowhere, and revelation and wisdom was a breath away. The Word is truly amazing!

Likewise, God gave us His Holy Spirit to help us sort things out, remind us of what Jesus taught, and lead us, especially during this time immediately prior to His Son's return. Jesus said in John 14:26: *"But the Advocate, the Holy Spirit, whom the Father will send in my name, will teach you all things and will remind you of everything I have said to you."* And consider the words of John in 1 John 2:27:

"As for you, the anointing [the Holy Spirit] *you received from Him remains in you, and you do not need anyone to teach you. But as his anointing teaches you about all things and as that anointing is real, not counterfeit—just as it has taught you, remain in him."* (clarification mine)

Jesus made the Father's intentions clear concerning His Holy Spirit when He said in Acts 1:5-9:

"For John baptized with water, but in a few days you will be baptized with the Holy Spirit." Then they gathered around him and asked him, *"Lord, are you at this time going to restore the kingdom to Israel?"* He said to them: *"It is not for you to know the times or dates the Father has set by his own authority. But you will receive power when the*

Holy Spirit comes on you; and you will be my witnesses in Jerusalem, and in all Judea and Samaria, and to the ends of the earth."

The same Holy Spirit that raised Yeshua from the dead would be poured out on all believers so there would be a proclamation of Messiah and a demonstration of the Kingdom in all the earth!

Paul also knew that a defining and distinguishing trait of the Kingdom would be the *power* of God displayed through all believers, drawing a needy world to the King. In 1 Corinthians 2:3-5, Paul proclaimed, *"And my message and my preaching were not in persuasive words of wisdom, but in demonstration of the Spirit and of power, that your faith should not rest on the wisdom of men, but on the power of God."*

During troubling times for Jewish and Gentile believers in Rome, Paul further pointed out that the Spirit helps us in our weakness, and even prays and intercedes for us when we are not sure what to do. Ever been there? In Romans 8:26-27, the apostle Paul wrote:

In the same way, the Spirit helps us in our weakness. We do not know what we ought to pray for, but the Spirit Himself intercedes for us through wordless groans. And He who searches our hearts knows the mind of the Spirit, because the Spirit intercedes for God's people in accordance with the will of God.

I could go on and on concerning what the Holy Spirit does for us, but here's a short list for you to check out later, if you wish. He guards us (Luke 12:11-12), gives us boldness (Acts 4:30-31), leads us (Luke 4:1-2), enables us to prophesy (Luke 1:67-68), talks with us and directs us (Acts 13:1-3), leads us into all the truth (John 16:12-14), strengthens us with His power (Ephesians 3:14-17), guides our words (Acts 16:6-9), assists in our sanctification and putting to death our sinful nature

(Romans 8:12-15), and helps us know God's thoughts (1 Corinthians 2:11-15).

Bottom line? We need the truth of God's Word and the leadership of the Holy Spirit to navigate life during these troubling times.

Discipline your mind to focus on the important things of life

The fourth and final key to being a worshiper in times of crisis, is to take control of our minds. We have all heard that when it comes to spiritual warfare the battlefield is in our mind, and it truly is. The enemy of our soul seeks daily to flood our thoughts with negativity, depression, doubt, worry, fear, accusations, and self-condemnation. He even tries to get us to make judgments and accusations towards God. We must discipline our minds, and like Paul said in 2 Corinthians 10:5, *"We demolish arguments and every pretension that sets itself up against the knowledge of God, and we take captive every thought to make it obedient to Christ."*

The Bible also says, *"For as he thinks within himself, so he is"* (Proverbs 23:7). We will ultimately say and do what we predominately think about on a daily basis. But even if we don't *actually* say or act on them, our thoughts are still who we really are on the inside. So it is imperative that we keep our minds focused on the Lord and out of the gutter!

Yeshua did this by keeping his mind on the Father, as in this Scripture:

> *Therefore Jesus answered and was saying to them, "Truly, truly, I say to you, the Son can do nothing of Himself, unless it is something He sees the Father doing; for whatever the Father does, these things the Son also does in like manner. For the Father loves the Son, and shows Him all things that He Himself is doing; and the Father will show Him greater works than these, so that you will marvel."* (John 5:19-20 NASB)

This is how our Savior walked in the power and authority while here on Earth. He kept His eyes on the Father and what He was doing, through prayer and His relationship with the Word of God and the Holy Spirit.

You might be asking yourself, "That's great information, but how do I actually discipline my mind and stay focused on the Lord?" Well, I'm glad you asked. Here are several truths to know and practice:

- Gird up your mind (1 Peter 1:13). As a soldier in Bible days would "gird up his garments" by gathering them tighter around him so he could fight more effectively, so we are to gather our thoughts and not just let our minds wander around the universe aimlessly. Cast down imaginations that are contrary to the knowledge of God (2 Corinthians 10:3-5).
- Set your mind on things above and not on things of the earth (Colossians 3:2).
- Renew your mind (Romans 12:2). The only way to do that is by getting into the Word of God and spending time reading, studying, and meditating on it.
- Set the filter of Philippians 4:8 on your mind. *"Finally, brothers and sisters, whatever is true, whatever is noble, whatever is right, whatever is pure, whatever is lovely, whatever is admirable—if anything is excellent or praiseworthy—think about such things."*
- Have a readiness of mind to search the Scriptures on all life matters. *"These were more noble than those in Thessalonica, in that they received the word with all readiness of mind, and searched the scriptures daily, whether those things were so."* (Acts 17:11 KJV)
- Keep your mind steadfast and focused on the Lord. *"You will keep in perfect peace those whose minds are steadfast, because they trust in you."* (Isaiah 26:3)

Actually, the best and most effective way I have found to renew my mind is to commit the Word of God to memory. The Scriptures have an amazing ability to transform our thinking and to get us moving in the right direction. When I was a new believer, I committed hundreds of verses to memory over the course of a year or two. The words that were planted in my soul kept me from danger, foolish choices, coarse joking and talk, destructive life patterns, and became my own words of choice. I found myself quoting the words back to myself when I would get confused or unsure which direction to take, and they became a comfort and guide for my life.

In John 14:9, Yeshua is speaking with Philip, one of His disciples and He says to him, *"he who has seen me has seen the Father."* It is my life goal to be able to say, "if you've seen me, you've seen my Messiah." Sound arrogant? I certainly hope not! True humility is found in worship, and my goal is to be one of those worshipers the Father is seeking who worship Him in spirit and in truth.

I encourage you to remember these strategies and let them help direct your life as you worship the King. You are a Kingdom citizen. You are an overcomer and a joint heir with Yeshua Himself! Live in His power and presence. All good things flow from Him as you worship Him in the midst of your daily experience. Worship is the key that opens every door. And for those of you who have not read my previous work, *Touching the Heart of God*, the experience of Abraham and Isaac on Mount Moriah—that of *obedience even unto death*—is much closer to true worship than any song sung with passion!

The real war of thrones is in full swing, in high definition with 3-D action and digital surround sound. It's called *life*. Yours can be successful and full of reward. The loser is the enemy of our soul, and he and all his followers will have terrible consequences for their rebellion—banishment from the presence of the King forever, surrounded by deep, thick, darkness and terror for all eternity. Yes, hell is real, the devil is real, demons are real, and Satan is warring against you—for real!

But take heart—the King of all kings is also engaged in this battle for your soul, and He has NEVER lost!

In closing, consider what the apostle John saw in a vision as he worshiped Yeshua on the Isle of Patmos, in the final day of the battle for the Throne:

> *I saw heaven standing open and there before me was a white horse, whose rider is called Faithful and True. With justice he judges and wages war. His eyes are like blazing fire, and on his head are many crowns. He has a name written on him that no one knows but he himself. He is dressed in a robe dipped in blood, and his name is the Word of God. The armies of heaven were following him, riding on white horses and dressed in fine linen, white and clean. Coming out of his mouth is a sharp sword with which to strike down the nations. "He will rule them with an iron scepter." He treads the winepress of the fury of the wrath of God Almighty. On his robe and on his thigh he has this name written: KING OF KINGS AND LORD OF LORDS.* (Revelation 19:11-16)

...a King is coming!

About the Authors

Paul Wilbur

Paul Wilbur was on his way to the opera houses and synagogues of the world when he met a young singer, at Indiana University Graduate School of Music, who would alter his life plans forever. Paul was determined to follow the footsteps of Metropolitan Opera star Richard Tucker, until he fell in love with Israel's Messiah back in March of 1977, while on a fishing trip with his friend Jerry Williams. From the first day, Paul knew his destiny was to sing, but the subject matter was to undergo a radical transformation. For more than forty years, Paul has traversed the globe with guitar in hand, singing and declaring the praises of Yeshua (Jesus) the Messiah, who set him free so many years ago. He has recorded too many projects to list here, performed them in multiple languages in seventy-five nations, has served on Messianic and church staffs for years, is an award-winning author, and an award-winning recording artist with Integrity Music. Paul has been married to the love of his life, Luanne, for nearly forty years. They have two married sons and a grandson.

Patrick McGuffin

Patrick McGuffin is a pastor, business leader, missionary, and author who brings his diverse background and experiences together in reaching many venues, both nationally and internationally. McGuffin, a University of Florida journalism graduate, spent the first part of his professional career publishing newspapers, ending that part of his life as president and publisher of nineteen newspapers. He is also a 1977 graduate of the Pointer Institute, a publishing institute open to the top journalists in the nation. The Orlando, Florida, based pastor has started a Christian newspaper in Ecuador and published four family magazines throughout Florida. He is a board member on two international Christian organizations—Heart of Titus Ministries, based in the United States, and Alejandro Arias International Ministries, based in Australia. He is married to his wife of nearly forty years, Sheila, and they have two married daughters and seven grandchildren.

NEED ADDITIONAL COPIES?

To order more copies of

 A **King** IS COMING

contact Certa Books

- Order online at:
  CertaBooks.com/AKingIsComing
- Call 855-77-CERTA or
- Email: info@CertaBooks.com

  Also available on Amazon.com

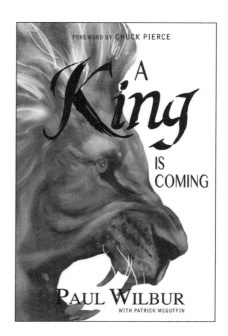

AWARD-WINNING BOOK BY PAUL WILBUR

To order copies of

TOUCHING
THE HEART OF GOD

contact Certa Books

- Order online at:
  CertaBooks.com/
  TouchingTheHeartOfGod
- Call 855-77-CERTA or
- Email: info@CertaBooks.com

  Also available on Amazon.com

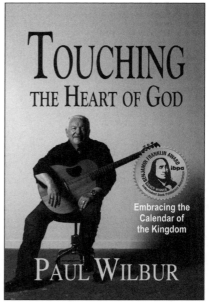

CERTA BOOKS
partner publishing